The
BIG WHEEL

THE
BIG WHEEL
Monte Carlo's Opulent Century

GEORGE W. HERALD

EDWARD D. RADIN

William Morrow
and Company
New York
1963

Acknowledgments

The authors wish to thank for their kind assistance Mr. Albert Lisimachio, director of the Palace Archives of His Serene Highness Prince Rainier of Monaco; Mr. Pierre Garuta of the Monaco Legation in Paris; Mr. René Novella, director of the Bibliothèque de Monaco; Mr. Ernest Pigazza, chief of the security services of the Monte Carlo Casino; and Mr. A. G. Bernard of the documentation service of the Sea Bathing Society, owners of the Monte Carlo Casino.

Valuable information, advice or suggestions were furnished by Prince Stanislas Radziwill, Mrs. Dolly Tvede-Radziwill, Mme. Marthe Bellando de Castro, Mr. and Mrs. Claude Samulon, Mrs. S. Pulman-Meury, Mrs. Dorothy Adelson and Miss Toni Howard.

Table of Contents

List of Illustrations

Mrs. Lily Langtry
Feodor Chaliapin
Sergei Diaghilev
Serge Lifar with Jean Cocteau, Darius Milhaud, and Nemtchinova
Serge Lifar with Pablo Picasso
Caroline Otero
Mata Hari
Sir Basil Zaharoff
Two drawings of Yvette Guilbert

between pages 152–153
Mrs. William Kissam Vanderbilt, Jr.
Mrs. O. H. P. Belmont
Consuelo Vanderbilt
Scott and Zelda Fitzgerald
Gabrielle Chanel
Chanel
The beach at Monte Carlo
Elsa Maxwell talking with Jack Warner
Sir Bernard and Lady Docker and her son
Ex-King Farouk
Tony and Sarah Churchill Beauchamp

between pages 216–217
Prince Rainier with Princess Grace and Princess Antoinette
Sir Winston Churchill in Nice with Aristotle Onassis
Mme. Maria Callas chatting with Sir Winston
Sir Winston at Cap Ferrat with Somerset Maugham
Aristotle Socrates Onassis
The Onassis pleasure yacht, *Christina*
Mr. Onassis and Mme. Callas
Mme. Benitez-Rexach with Georges Simenon
Le Moineau
Greta Garbo
The Duke of Edinburgh
Fortuneteller in Hôtel de Paris

The
BIG WHEEL

CHAPTER 1

A Queen Is Born

The Factory is now one hundred years old.

It may be best not to repeat this in the presence of His Serene Highness Prince Rainier III of Monaco. And it may be equally discreet not to mention it to Aristotle Socrates Onassis, multimillionaire owner of a huge tanker fleet and head of Monaco's Société des Bains de Mer et Cercle des Étrangers. It is not that these two men object to the venerable age of the Factory; in fact, they are proud of it. But they may not like the irreverent Factory nickname that some players use in referring to the dowager queen of all gambling places, the Monte Carlo Casino.

It was in February, 1863, when the present structure, much smaller and simpler then, flung open its doors for the first time. There were no brass bands, no imposing list of royal dignitaries, no cheering populace, and especially, no surging and impatient throng of waiting gamblers.

There was the contractor, hopeful now that he might be paid, and a few curious Monégasque citizens, still unbelieving that anybody would put up a building on the bleak rock that had served so long as the communal garbage dump. And up on the roof, taking turns at placing telescope to eye, were several directors peering seaward and wondering if the steamer from Nice might come. There were always so many ifs connected with the erratic and ramshackle little coastal vessel; if the captain happened to be sober and wanted to make the trip, if the vessel had not broken down, if there were enough passengers on board to make the trip worth while. The only other way into the isolated principality was by mail coach, a four-hour bone-jolting ride over boulder-strewn ruts, and since there were no hotel rooms in Monaco then, this meant a return trip the same day, eight hours of self-imposed torture that made even a compulsive gambler blanch.

But if the opening was inauspicious and virtually unnoticed, nevertheless a queen had been born, one who showed her regal strain in the way she persevered through newspaper attacks, denunciations from pulpits, blackmail and extortion plots; and she became, more than a gambling place, more than a resort, a highly respected and beloved international institution, so much so that a German general during World War II declared the Monte Carlo Casino an historical monument not to be damaged.

In the parlance of the gambling fraternity, the Monte Carlo Casino is the Big Wheel, the greatest of them all, and the envy of the others. Whether true or not, owners of gambling clubs at Las Vegas like to boast that their combined play in one month is more than is wagered in an entire year at Monte Carlo; yet they would happily give up a month's receipts if a portion of the patina of Monte Carlo's elegance, and its aura of respectability, could rub off on their places. To many people all over the world a trip to Monte Carlo is a wish-fulfillment, a dream that has come true. Many women who would hesitate to go to a gambling club eagerly enter the salons at Monte Carlo.

One need not be a psychologist to understand this, for

they are walking into history; here was the playground of kings, the favorite resort of fabled beauties and men of enormous wealth. In these salons cavorted the madcap grand dukes of Russia, showering gold like confetti, while their serfs starved and finally revolted. On the boards of the opera house appeared the finest talent, and gala premières presented operas and ballets to the world. And it is still possible to rub shoulders there with some of the remaining members of royalty, to view statesmen, notables from many fields and movie stars, to mingle with persons whose photographs adorn the society pages, as well as with strumpets, pimps and a fleeing embezzler or two.

And in its climb to its unique pinnacle, the casino brought along with it all of Monaco, converting the barren and useless rock into an exquisite jewel of breathtaking beauty. Many visitors upon their first view involuntarily exclaim, "I don't believe it." It is difficult in this pragmatic world of today to be confronted suddenly with a fairy-tale princedom that does exist in real life.

The story of Monte Carlo's century is a reflection of the eras it passed through, distorted by its own limitations, but just the same mirroring certain aspects of the time, and keeping up-to-date in its faithful reproduction. With more American tourists arriving since the marriage of Prince Rainier and the Princess Grace, the former Grace Kelly of Philadelphia and Hollywood, the casino still strives to be a faithful mirror, and so there are dice tables in the salon and slot machines in the lobby.

It is proper to refer to the Monte Carlo Casino as a queen, for even though it was Prince Charles III who brought gambling to the Rock, and for whom Monte Carlo is named, it was a woman, his mother Princess Caroline, who suggested that a concession for a gambling casino be granted as a means of adding to their meager income.

The Grimaldi family is one of the longest ruling dynasties in the modern world. For generation after generation they clung with amazing tenacity to their throne. Ruling over a principality that even when it had more land was still too small to be viable as a country, the throne was the most threadbare in Europe. Monégasques sang a song which told the story; they lived on a rock and could neither sow nor reap. They referred to their homeland simply as the Rock. At the same time this helped the Grimaldis keep their royal embellishments, for the brutal truth is that no neighboring country thought that the Rock was worth while taking.

Although newspapers always report that François Blanc founded the Monte Carlo Casino, this is not so. He was the fifth person to hold the concession. He did not enter the picture until after the dismal opening and the concessionaires, like their predecessors, were virtually bankrupt. And like the proverbial hero of an operetta, Blanc arrived just in time to save the bankrupt throne and start the Monte Carlo Casino off on its brilliant career.

The Grimaldis had been dealt what seemed to be a death blow by the Turin Peace Treaty of 1861, which brought to a close a war waged together by France and Sardinia against Austria, and which drove the Hapsburgs from northern Italy. Tiny Monaco was an innocent victim in the midst of the battle. At the end of the war, possibly spurred by secret agents, its two largest townships, Menton and Roquebrune, the only ones that were able to pay taxes from their thriving orange and olive groves, asked to be annexed by France, and were gladly welcomed into the Second Empire. In one gulp France had taken away four fifths of Monaco's territory. What was left is the present-day Monaco, a small coastal strip of 368 acres that could fit comfortably inside New York City's Central Park, or just about fill London's Hyde Park.

As a sop to stricken Prince Charles, France agreed to pay

him three million francs in cash for the territory, but how he was supposed to maintain a throne on the barren rock once the money was used up was not mentioned, although France solemnly guaranteed his throne in the treaty. Prince Charles, still hopeful that the casino might amount to something, also managed to get France to agree to construct a new highway and a railroad line, connecting Nice and Monaco. When completed, these would end the principality's isolation. The railroad line was to become worth its weight in gold to Monaco, far outstripping the value of the land taken away from it.

It was at Prince Charles's suggestion that the harried owners of the new casino building sought out Blanc and asked him to take over. They haggled over terms, wanting more than he would pay, until he contemptuously dumped 1,700,-000 francs on a table and told them to take it or leave it. The sight of the cash was too much for the holders of the concession; they took the money and signed without any further arguments.

It was Blanc who organized the curiously named Société des Bains de Mer et Cercle des Étrangers, the Sea Bathing Society and Circle of Foreigners, the corporation which owns the casino. There was no beach in the principality at that time. The "Foreigners" in the title referred to the fact that no native of Monaco would be allowed to gamble in the casino. The present management of the casino considers that its official history began when Blanc took over in late April, 1863, and the first roulette wheel spun under his management several weeks later.

François Blanc also founded a dynasty in Monte Carlo. First he, and then his son Camille, ruled the casino with an iron hand for sixty years, until well after World War I, and it was they who created the image of the casino that still exists.

François Blanc was fifty-seven years old when he took over the concession, and he was, to put it mildly, a controversial figure. He has been called a "modern magician and a financial genius." Others simply termed him "a scourge of humanity."

Born near Bordeaux where his father had been a tax collector, he went to work at the age of fourteen as a dishwasher in a restaurant, and later worked as a waiter in gambling clubs. He started speculating on the stock market, made money and finally opened a brokerage office in Bordeaux with his twin brother Louis. They seemed to be phenomenally astute, and their own purchases uncannily predicted the rise and fall of stocks. They had amassed a fortune of almost a half-million francs when their secret was discovered. The brothers had bribed postal clerks in charge of the semaphore telegraph between Paris and Bordeaux, and were being supplied with the daily closing prices on the Paris stock exchange a good thirty minutes before these figures reached the other Bordeaux brokers. They were sentenced to a brief seven months in prison for fraud and bribery.

The brothers now turned honest, moved to Luxembourg and opened a gambling casino. François met a girl there and became the father of two sons, Charles and Camille. No marriage was ever announced, and there is no record of the mother's name. Several years later Blanc was registered as a widower with two sons.

Many West German princelings of that era were constantly in debt, and in August, 1840, Count Philipp of Homburg offered the Blanc brothers a concession to operate a casino in his state. It was attractive to the brothers because the town was known for its curative waters, and they soon transformed it into an international resort favored by wealthy Englishmen, French and Russians. Feodor Dostoevski was a frequent visitor. Louis Blanc died there, and François carried on alone.

He hired Marie Hensal, a strikingly beautiful girl, daughter of a local cobbler, to take care of his two young sons, and soon fell in love with her. He offered to marry her if she would get a good education at his expense, and he sent her to a Paris boarding school. After two years of grooming, he decided that she now could appear at his side in his fashionable casino. They were married on June 20, 1854, and they unabashedly announced the birth of a daughter five months later.

Blanc knew that he was operating on limited time, that Bismarck would succeed in forming a united Germany, ending the petty states, and that the Iron Chancellor was a foe of gambling. He had watched the floundering attempts being made in Monaco to establish a casino there and was interested, though he wanted to wait until the Nice railroad was completed, ending Monaco's isolation, before stepping in. But Prince Charles's dwindling fortune and his impatience, since he had received no money from any of the four previous owners of the casino, forced Blanc's hand, and he bought the casino.

Blanc brought both experience and ample funds with him. Although nearby Nice and Cannes were building up as winter resorts, many visitors there did not even know that there was a casino at Monte Carlo because the previous owners had been reluctant to spend money for advertising. France had banned all gambling, but there was some talk that casinos might open in neighboring northern Italy. A violent attack on gambling soon broke out there. Leaflets were distributed, and posters put up denouncing gaming houses as dens of vice. Prime Minister Cavour, bowing to the popular clamor, banned the opening of any casinos in northern Italy. It wasn't until years later that he learned that this campaign had been ordered and financed by François Blanc.

The original Sea Bathing Society was organized with 12

million francs' capital, and 30,000 shares were issued. Blanc
kept 18,000 shares for himself and put another 4,000 in his
wife's name. He had no difficulty selling the rest. One of the
earliest investors in the casino was Cardinal Pecci, who later
became Pope Leo XIII.

Prince Charles granted a new concession to run for fifty
years, and received in exchange a guaranteed payment of
50,000 francs a year, plus 10 per cent of the net profits. For
the first time, the Grimaldis now had a steady income. Blanc
also assumed the cost of paying the police and the army of
120 men. This practice later was dropped. He also offered
Prince Charles an additional private allowance of 2,000 francs
a week, as a gesture of good will. The prince thanked him
and requested the payment to be made in two bank notes
of 1,000 francs each. Blanc was surprised because payments
usually were made in gold pieces, rolls of fifty louis d'or,
equal to 1,000 francs, in a package. When he asked why not
in gold pieces, the ruling prince bluntly told him that he
feared that the rolls might not contain the full count. Prince
Charles was well aware of Blanc's early career.

But he was to be happily surprised by Blanc, who kept his
word on everything. Blanc hired fifty stagecoaches to transport guests from Cannes to Nice, where they could board
a flotilla of steamboats he had chartered to bring gamblers
to Monaco.

The original concessionaires had purchased about one
hundred acres of land in Monaco, paying the trifling sum
of twenty-two centimes a yard for it. They later had offered
acres of it free to anybody who would build a house on the
casino rock, so that gamblers would have a place to sleep if
they wanted to stay overnight, but the land was considered
so worthless that nobody would even take it as a gift. Today
that land is among the highest priced in the world.

Blanc did more than operate the casino; he planned a town

and began to build streets, hotels and villas. And he brought in mountains of soil to cover the bare rock and an army of gardeners to plant flowers, trees and shrubs.

Within a short time, Jean-Marie Saint-Germain, a prominent reporter, wrote: "That which was the most arid has become fertile, the desert is peopled, the bare rock has become an immense bouquet. Civilization with all its luxuries has embellished this solitude. Large avenues bordered with green trees and white houses stretch forth in all directions over this superb tableland; veritably a gleaming jewel held tightly in a frame of mountains."

This new town, occupying almost one half of Monaco, was named Monte Carlo in honor of the ruling prince.

Blanc also was fair to the players and increased their chances of winning. The previous concessionaires had introduced a second zero on the roulette wheel which, oddly, is still used by the casinos in Nevada. This sharply increases the advantage of the house to the detriment of the players, but Blanc eliminated this second zero. In his first year of operation he was able to show a profit of 800,000 francs, and three years later this rose to over two million francs.

The railroad company, which had been moving at a leisurely pace since it saw little use for the spur line it was constructing between Nice and Monaco, now realized its potentials, and rushed additional work crews there. President James de Rothschild of the Paris-Lyon-Mediterranean Railroad opened service on the line in October, 1868, two years ahead of schedule.

The opening of the railroad and the increasing popularity of the Riviera as a winter resort started a gold rush in Monte Carlo. Land values zoomed as packed trains pulled in almost every hour. The gaming rooms were crowded from morning to night, and the casino revenues kept pace.

The casino promptly came under severe attack. Neighboring Nice became jealous of the competing resort, and its newspapers opened a violent campaign against the gambling house. Monte Carlo was denounced as being responsible for a wave of suicides that seemed to have been decimating the population. One story claimed that the bodies of ruined gamblers were piling up in the grottoes below the casino rock. Others stated that boats secretly left the port of Monaco twice a week loaded to the gunwales with corpses that were dumped out into the sea several miles offshore.

These stories also spread to the United States. An American woman noticed the windowless carts used by Monaco's dogcatchers and asked what they were. Her companion replied that these carts went around every morning to pick up the suicides lying in the streets. The woman took him seriously and wrote an indignant letter to her home paper. The story was picked up and published all over the country.

There were, of course, genuine suicides by gamblers. One afternoon after a man had tried to shoot himself and the gun had been wrested from him, Blanc rushed up to the distraught man and shouted at him, "Sir, you are no gentleman. If you wish to shoot yourself, please do so at home and not in my casino gardens." On the more practical side, the sale of all firearms and poisons was forbidden in Monaco. Even today pharmacies there do not sell any poisonous material. Hotel detectives were ordered to search the baggage of all visitors and remove the bullets from any firearms. In addition, instructions were issued to trusted employees to thrust a wad of money into the pocket of any suicide before police were summoned, so that the claim could be made that the death was due to a love affair and not gaming losses.

A swindler promptly took advantage of this order. Two guards patrolling the Jardins Exotiques found a body covered with blood. They quickly stuffed the pockets with money and hurried away, to make their official discovery later. When they did return, the body was gone. The man had daubed himself with tomato paste, which, in the semi-darkness, the guards had mistaken for blood.

Blanc also had troubles much closer at home. The native Monégasques were embittered; they were not sharing in the golden flood since Blanc had brought with him experienced croupiers from his Homburg casino, which was closed during the winter. His detectives heard rumors that the people were planning to sack the casino. Since Prince Charles's income from the casino had risen with the profits, Blanc induced the prince in 1869 to abolish all taxes for native citizens. It was a master stroke; not only did it make the Grimaldis popular with their subjects, but Blanc was hailed as a benefactor, and the natives prayed for the continuing success of the casino.

Blanc, by now, dominated Monaco, and he wanted the soldiers to salute his wife when she appeared on the street. The army was unwilling until Blanc, who paid their wages, said he would hire a new army of 120 men. Marie Blanc, the former cobbler's daughter, soon was being saluted smartly whenever she appeared on the streets.

The press attacks continued, and many ministers also preached against the casino. This was the Victorian era, and the prudishness of that court had spread in many areas. Queen Victoria, who spent part of her winters on the Riviera, usually started her season in France and finished it in Italy. When the directors of the casino learned that her carriage was due to pass through Monaco, they hurried to the border with an armload of flowers as a good-will gesture to welcome her on her ride through the principality. When she learned the identity of the visitors, she refused the flowers and closed the doors of her carriage until it had passed through Monaco.

Two nimble-witted blackmailers tried to take advantage of this hostility to the casino and rented a billboard outside of Nice on the way to Monte Carlo. They hired an artist to

paint four murals on it. The first showed the brilliantly
lighted entrance to Monte Carlo. The second showed dozens
of suicides either writhing on the ground or hanging from
lamp posts in the casino gardens. The third featured a widow,
surrounded by small children, blaming the casino for her
plight, while the fourth portrayed Prince Charles receiving
bags full of gold and bank notes from François Blanc.

Stories and reproductions of the murals appeared in newspapers everywhere, and Blanc decided to pay off, but changed
his mind when the blackmailers demanded one million
francs. His detectives learned that the men were living in
a cheap hotel at Villefranche and were running out of money.
They soon reduced their demands to 25,000 francs, but Blanc
simply waited them out. When they were unable to pay their
rent for the billboard, the space was taken over by a wine
company, which painted out the murals to promote its own
products.

Some of the newspaper attacks died down when Blanc
placed important officials on his payroll. He spent a half-
million francs a year on the press. The editor of a Paris paper
received 25,000 francs a year solely to mention the weather
every day in Monte Carlo; it was what he was not mentioning that Blanc was buying.

Four Paris gossip writers, angry because they were not on
the payroll, came up with a successful scheme of their own.
They built six fake bombs and promised bribes to several
guards to smuggle them into the casino and pretend that they
had found them under the roulette tables. Since this occurred
while players were present, the story soon spread that they
had been real bombs. The four men then went to Blanc and
demanded 25,000 francs to hush up the story. Blanc showed
them the fake bombs and said it must have been a practical
joke by some player. The quartet promptly accused Blanc
of having the fake bombs made to cover up the real story. The

worried roulette king paid them off, and they left at once for Paris. One of the disgruntled guards, who had not been paid, later told Blanc the true story.

Blanc also contributed money in other ways to buy good will for the casino. He loaned 4,800,000 francs to architect Charles Garnier to help finance the construction of the Paris Opera, and contributed two million francs toward the payment of France's war debt to Bismarck.

In 1876, François Blanc, by now a friend and confidant of kings, queens and the aristocracy of Europe, was able to marry a daughter to Prince Constantin Radziwill, and he brought his royal son-in-law into the business. The wedding was attended by many members of the Russian and German nobility. Blanc died a year later and left a fortune of 72 million francs, the equivalent then of 45 million dollars, most of it made in Monte Carlo.

There was no change in policy, or any break in the upward sweep of Monte Carlo, as his son Camille took over the active management. There were many changes, though, in the casino building. The original structure had been rather modest and plain, but it was now completely redesigned, its famous bulbous green-gold dome being added, along with four Oriental minarets, so that it is today a mixture of classic Greek, Moorish, Gothic and French Second Empire styles. The added west wing contained the Monte Carlo Opera House, which reached its glory under the watchful eye of the first American princess of Monaco, the former Alice Heine. The new east wing provided space for the famous private salons, the *salons privés,* limited to those of aristocracy or of great wealth. There are eleven salons in the casino.

Bertie, the Prince of Wales, started the royal rush there when the resort became his favorite roistering place. He gave a boost up the ladder to César Ritz, the great hotel man, who later managed London's noted Savoy Hotel. Ritz was

thirty years old when he was named director of the Grand
Hotel in Monte Carlo, and because the Prince of Wales liked
him, he began to stay there, and the hotel became a favorite
place for many visiting kings. Ritz brought in the great chef,
Auguste Escoffier, and during a 10-year span these two men
did almost as much for Monte Carlo as the casino. Ritz revo-
lutionized the hotel business with his policy that the customer, whether he was royalty or not, always was king, and
his deft service and the superb food served at the Grand Hotel
became internationally famous.

In 1887, the enemies of the casino thought their prayers
had been answered when a series of tremors shook the Riviera, and even the solid casino rock quivered. A Mardi Gras
ball had been held in the casino theater on the night of
February 23, and it was not until six o'clock the following
morning that the band played its final number. The casino
square was still filled with a gay crowd of masked revelers
when the ground trembled beneath their feet, and from the
hills of Castellar and La Turbie came the deafening noise
of houses collapsing.

Panic broke out in front of the casino. An Englishman,
who still was in his costume as Caesar, mounted the casino
steps and began a sermon. A second tremor sent the crowd
to their knees in prayer, but an American broke the spell
when he shouted to his wife, "Let's get out of here and catch
the next train." The crowd began streaming to the station,
only to learn that the tracks had been torn up.

Hundreds of people came rushing out of the hotels in their
night clothes. Several walls of the Grand Hotel were shattered. Mrs. Ritz later said, "After the first seismic shock, bed-
lam broke out in the hotel. The ladies in their nightgowns
and hair curlers came rushing down the staircases, not without having hastily grabbed as many of their jewels as they
could lay their hands on. But as many of the women trem-

bled as much as the building, their diamonds, rubies and emeralds slipped from their hands and rolled down the steps in front of them in a scintillating cascade."

The frightened crowd made a mad dash when a four-in-hand coach appeared. It contained King Karl of Württemberg; he was not fleeing, he wanted to go to his yacht and watch the earthquake from there. His example gave two wealthy Belgians an idea; they offered a coachman 5,000 francs to take them to Villefranche. He was too frightened to take to the road, but quick-witted enough to demand, and get, 1,000 francs for letting them crawl under his vehicle to be out of the way of any falling debris.

Elsewhere on the square an elderly English noblewoman tried to climb a 45-foot-high palm tree in front of the casino because she had lost her wig and did not want to be seen without it. A furniture manufacturer from Cologne kept running around with his mistress, shouting, "I am in Geneva, I am in Geneva." He had slipped away to the resort after telling his wife he had to go to Switzerland on business.

A baroness, the wife of the Governor of the Bank of France, publicly pledged that she would never set foot in the casino again, and would build a church with her present winnings if she survived the terror. The last severe tremor was felt in Monte Carlo at eight thirty that morning.

The following year the baroness was back in Monte Carlo. Asked if she had built the promised church, she shook her head and replied, "I thought it over and gave six candles instead. After all, it was only a very small earthquake."

Although Monte Carlo itself got off comparatively lightly, 350 people were killed along the Riviera.

But neither earthquakes nor denunciations stopped the onward rush of the casino; its profits were in the millions of francs yearly.

James Gordon Bennett, owner of the New York *Herald,*

lured many of his countrymen to Monte Carlo. He had started the famous Paris edition of his paper and in the 1870's finally moved to Europe. He bought a villa on the Riviera and found himself lonely for fellow Americans; not too many were appearing then on the Côte d'Azur. To stimulate them into coming, he began publishing a Riviera column in the Paris edition, filling it with the names of prominent people vacationing there and sprinkling in as many American names as he could. Since the paper was bought by many Americans visiting Europe, they considered it a sign of social recognition to be mentioned in the column, and began heading for the Riviera. Not long afterward he was entertaining such guests at his villa as the Morgans, the Vanderbilts, the Drexels, the Biddles and the Wanamakers.

One of Bennett's favorite restaurants in Monte Carlo was the Café Riche, where he liked to dine on the terrace. The management decided one day that only drinks would be served on the terrace, that all meals had to be eaten inside the café. Bennett became angered, bought the restaurant, summoned his favorite waiter, an Egyptian called Ciro, and handed the business over to him. The name was changed to Ciro's Restaurant and Bennett mentioned it so often in his paper that it became the rage of the social set. Ciro soon expanded his business, opening branches in many European cities.

Bennett's friend, J. P. Morgan, is the only man who ever refused to play at the Monte Carlo Casino because the stakes were not high enough. The maximum bet then was 12,000 francs and Morgan wanted it increased to 20,000. When Blanc refused to do this, Morgan snorted, "Twelve thousand francs. I have no time to lose such ridiculous amounts." He once reproached Charles M. Schwab, then head of Carnegie Steel, for having spent a gay night in the bars of Monte Carlo. When Schwab retorted that he was committing his sins openly and not behind locked doors, Morgan thumped his hand down on the table and replied, "That's what doors are there for, my friend."

The most eccentric American millionaire on the Riviera at that time was a man named Neal, a beauty cream inventor. He had an artificial moon constructed that slowly turned around his house during the night, and he refused to summon servants by ringing a bell. He always fired a pistol, and the number of shots denoted whether he wanted the chambermaid, the valet or the butler. He frequently gave parties in his own honor and had an agency supply him with sixty to eighty guests at a time. In return for the food and drink, they had to listen to him expound his views at the dinner table and laugh at his jokes. From time to time, he would descend on the Hôtel Hermitage with his retinue. And when he entered alone, they had to jump to their feet and bow low before him.

Three American socialites, Porter Clark, Richard Davies and Jack Reynolds, enjoyed practical jokes. One of their favorites was to pay large sums to coachmen to rent their rigs for the night, and take their places. As soon as each had unsuspecting passengers aboard, they would set out in a wild Ben-Hur type of race down Monte Carlo's hilly streets.

Camille Blanc did not mind the antics of his wealthy guests. The casino had constructed the beautiful Hôtel de Paris next door to the casino, and it became a gathering place for the famous. The guest list for a stag dinner listed, among others, W. K. Vanderbilt, Ignace Paderewski, the Prince of Saschen-Meiningen, David Lloyd George, Grand Duke Boris, the Aga Khan, Henri Bernstein and Lord Rothmere.

Blanc was the first to introduce automobile competitions. The cars were displayed in the morning on the terrace in front of the casino, and then paraded in the afternoon before a jury who judged the elegance of the vehicles and the drivers.

Since Blanc would not admit that anything might be second-rate in his little bit of paradise, all the contestants were winners. They won either a Grand Prix, a Premier Prix, or a Prix d'Honneur.

The famous beauty, Gaby Deslys, collected more trophies than anybody else. The dancer was the mistress of King Emmanuel of Portugal, and among the jewels she collected from him was a 17-row pearl necklace, not only perfectly matched, but each pearl the size of a small grape. She danced one winter professionally in Monte Carlo, and before she appeared on the stage, the manager took her aside and told her not to forget to bow to the front table on the left when she came out. Seated at that table were the King of Sweden, the King of Denmark, the King of Portugal and the King of Württemberg. A South American coffee king, Señor Unzue, was so enchanted with her dancing that he sent a flower basket up to her room in the Hôtel de Paris. Instead of being filled with exotic flowers, it had a rare bloom of its own; it was filled with 20-dollar gold pieces. Gaby sent him a note thanking him for his friendly gesture.

The Monte Carlo Casino no longer had to buy off the press to prevent fake suicide stories. The large newspapers of the world, the press associations, all had reporters stationed there to keep their readers informed on the latest news, the gossip, the clothes, the guests. No royal court was as closely watched or discussed. A gambling casino with its salons decorated with gilded frescoes, gilded coats of arms, and gilded sculptures of giant women, of naked children, of Nubian slaves brandishing heavy golden candelabra, and, on the ceiling of one room, of nude women smoking cigars, had become an institution, a queen.

CHAPTER 2

Kings and "Queens"

Although Queen Victoria considered Monte Carlo a den of iniquity, and would order the curtains of her railroad car closed whenever her train steamed through Monaco on its way to a more staid Riviera resort, this feeling was not shared by her eldest son Bertie, the Prince of Wales, who later became Edward VII.

For some thirty years, during the long reign of his mother, the prince cavorted in Monaco, indulging his awesome appetite for women, food and pleasure. After he succeeded to the throne, the official records show no visit of Edward VII to Monte Carlo, but he continued to make frequent secret trips to the Côte d'Azur, using his favorite pseudonym of Baron Renfrew. And there are still elderly men in Monte Carlo, sitting quietly in the sun, who joyfully shout, "Papa," when shown his photograph.

Edward VII was not the only ruling monarch who found surcease from arduous affairs of state under Monte Carlo's balmy skies or in the smoke-filled *salons privés* of the casino. A few came accompanied by their queens, the genuine blue-blood variety, but most of them preferred the queens of the demimonde, who had a hierarchy of their own. But the activities of a few of the real queens also added gaiety to the season.

In recent years there have been so many people who falsely claim that they are love children of royal romances that the late E. Phillips Oppenheim scornfully referred to them as the "Society of Royal Bastards." He described them as men and women who "felt compelled to label themselves bastards and their mother a whore in order to claim a few drops of royal blood." Most of these pretenders have been very careful in the choice of their father, selecting only the more celebrated royal women-chasers such as Edward VII, Grand Duke Michael, Leopold II of Belgium and various Hapsburgs.

It was one of the Hapsburgs, Emperor Franz Josef of Austria and King of Hungary, who had the unusual distinction of being the only important reigning monarch to be the victim of a blackmail plot at Monte Carlo.

The aging emperor, who was well known for his roving eye, had no difficulty at all in spotting a young Greek goddess named Ilona. She was a raven-haired beauty with a perfect figure to match. What the ruler did not know was that Ilona had been installed in her suite in the Hôtel de Paris, where he preferred to stay, by a blackmail gang headed by Carter Aubrey, an Englishman, who had furnished her with money, jewels and a wardrobe in keeping with her surroundings. Her orders were simple; she was to seduce Emperor Franz Josef. In view of his reputation, no difficulty at all was anticipated.

Not long after his arrival Emperor Franz Josef noticed Ilona, and his aide-de-camp was dispatched to the girl's side with a message that His Majesty would be delighted if she accepted an invitation to dine with him that evening at his apartment.

The blackmailers were equally delighted, but complications quickly arose. They soon discovered that the monarch was not quite alone; he had brought with him to Monte Carlo his favorite mistress of that winter, a statuesque blonde named Gussy. With Gussy present, the dinner that night with Ilona was just that, a dinner. Other dates were made, but Gussy managed to get wind of them and put in an appearance.

By now the blackmailers were getting desperate; they had made a heavy cash investment without results. One night while Gussy was taking a stroll on a dark street, she was seized by several members of the gang, who dragged her into a waiting coach. They wanted to rush her across the border into Italy and hold her there long enough for Ilona to accomplish her mission. The husky woman, however, proved to be too much for her would-be abductors, and she escaped from the carriage.

Although Gussy warned her lover that a plot was aimed at him, the monarch disregarded her advice. Ilona succeeded in arranging a daytime tryst in a secluded villa west of Monte Carlo. Franz Josef came alone, and when he entered the salon, Ilona was waiting for him clad in a filmy negligee. She lost little time in throwing herself at him, and a few minutes later Aubrey and two accomplices burst into the room, with the Englishman acting the part of an outraged husband, threatening to call authorities. The royal visitor shrugged, told Aubrey to suit himself and left the villa.

When he returned to his hotel, Gussy was waiting for him. He explained what had happened, and the practical blonde promptly came up with a solution. She advised the emperor to leave immediately for Vienna. Once he was safely across the border, there was little that anybody could do. Several hours later Franz Josef and Gussy were on a special train. When Aubrey called at the hotel that night to talk things over, his prey was gone.

The cheeky Englishman evidently had more nerve than brains. He turned up in Vienna the following week, presented his card to the king's chamberlain and requested an audience with the ruler, stating that it was an urgent private matter with which the emperor was familiar. What Aubrey had failed to consider was that Franz Josef was an absolute monarch in his realm. He promptly had the Englishman arrested and placed in isolated custody in a fortress deep in southern Hungary. After some three months of lonely incarceration, Aubrey wrote a letter of apology and agreed to forget the Ilona incident in return for his freedom. He was released. Information about the gang was supplied to Monaco officials; the members were rounded up and expelled from the principality.

For the sake of appearances, Franz Josef's trips to Monte Carlo were supposed to be visits to Empress Elizabeth, who always vacationed there, but they went their separate ways. Sissy, as she was called, always rented the ground floor in the right wing of the Hôtel du Cap Martin, from where she had a splendid view of the entire coast between Monaco and Bordighera. Her bedroom had special reinforced ceiling timbers installed for a swing that she kept above her gilt bed. She was a trained acrobat and would work out on the swing each morning in order to retain her slim figure.

While her husband carried on with his love affairs, Sissy was busy with her own. Her first lover was Hungarian Count Andrassy, and court circles always considered him the actual father of Archduke Rudolf, the heir to the Hapsburg throne, who later died mysteriously at Mayerling. She also had an affair with an attaché assigned to the British Embassy in Vienna. After he was recalled to London, she often visited him there, accompanied by Mme. Larisch, her lady-in-waiting. She later gave birth to his daughter in Normandy.

Raoul Gunsbourg, who directed the Monte Carlo Opera

for many years, claimed that he had learned the real story of the tragedy at Mayerling from Mme. Schratt, the emperor's best-known mistress, who had a villa near Monaco.

She told him that Franz Josef knew of his wife's infidelities, but for reasons of state had to remain silent. He hated Archduke Rudolf, the heir who was not his son, and the young man, in return, heartily disliked the king. Once while they were on a deer hunt together, a bullet fired by Rudolf narrowly missed the ruler, and although those on the shoot considered it an accident, Franz Josef was not so certain.

The archduke also was a notorious woman-chaser, rather indiscriminate in his choices. He picked what pleased his eye, a countess one night, a scullery maid another. But most of the women he pursued had one thing in common; they usually were married. The archduke got a special delight out of cuckolding husbands.

According to Mme. Schratt's story, two members of the palace staff, a coachman and a gamekeeper, requested an audience with the emperor. Both men complained to him that the archduke had seduced their wives. The gamekeeper was particularly bitter and is supposed to have exclaimed, "If I were a nobleman, I would know how to avenge myself."

Franz Josef was said to have replied, "I don't think this is a matter of social rank."

A few weeks later they shot Rudolf in the head through an open window of his hunting lodge at Mayerling. Marie Vetsera, his mistress of the moment, was killed when she threw herself against his body in a vain attempt to save him.

The death of the couple was long considered by the public a suicide pact. To substantiate her story, Mme. Schratt pointed out that the Pope would not grant absolution to a suicide, but when the emperor gave his word to the pontiff that it had been a case of murder, absolution was given. She said the coachman and the gamekeeper later received a large sum of money from Franz Josef to leave Europe for South America.

Kaiser Wilhelm II made only one trip to Monte Carlo, arriving aboard his yacht, *Hohenzollern*. He came for just one purpose, to play roulette, and in his typical fashion he had prepared himself to win. He had heard of a system worked out by Dr. Schott, a mathematics professor at Heidelberg University. He had bought the system from Dr. Schott and appeared incognito at the casino to try it out. The kaiser lost 100,000 francs that night. He never returned to Monte Carlo, and Dr. Schott never received further promotion at the university.

Czar Nicholas II, a frequent visitor to Monte Carlo, lived an almost monastic life there in sharp contrast with the conduct of the roistering grand dukes. Part of it was due to a justified fear of assassination by Anarchists; he was heavily guarded during each stay. But the czarina, who was an extremely jealous woman, also helped keep him on a short leash by playing on local police fears of such an incident. She was an avid reader of the Anarchist weeklies, which were surprisingly well informed about his private affairs. He had a weakness for dancers. As soon as she learned from her reading the name of his latest interest, she would advise police to deport the girl because the Anarchists might be using her, and the frustrated czar would have to prowl around for a new find.

On one occasion, a maid discovered a nude unkempt stranger sunbathing in the garden of the czar's villa. Her screams brought guards racing up. The vagabond explained that he had thought the villa was unoccupied and had removed his clothes to delouse himself. The relieved czarina sent the bewildered hobo on his way with a large hamper of food, one of her husband's hand-tailored suits and a well-filled purse.

Because Grand Duke Vladimir had been wounded twice in previous attempts on his life, a police inspector was assigned as his personal bodyguard each time he came to the Riviera. While upstairs one night, the grand duke heard a crackling noise on the ground floor of his villa. Arming himself with a candelabra, he quietly crept down the stairs, and saw a crouching figure in a corner of the darkened hall.

The grand duke rushed forward and crashed the heavy weapon down upon the skull of the crouching man. It was only after he had put on the lights that he discovered that he had killed the police inspector, who was busy unwrapping a sandwich. The incident was hushed up with Vladimir paying 200,000 francs to keep the story out of the papers. The family of the dead man was informed that he had been killed when a piece of rock accidently fell on his head.

To prevent any further accidents of that sort, guard duty was assumed by members of the Okhrana, the Russian secret service. As a further precaution, plain-clothes men were sent from Saint Petersburg to scrutinize visitors arriving by train. All recognized terrorists were not permitted to leave the station, but had to take the next train returning to Nice.

Surprised Monaco officials learned that not all terrorists were bushy-haired bomb-throwers. They received word that hotel reservations had been made for Prince Victor Nakashidze, a relative of the Romanovs. Following the customary protocol, a red carpet was rolled out at the station, and a delegation in morning coats and top hats welcomed the prince as he stepped off the train.

One of the Okhrana agents dashed up in the midst of the ceremonies and demanded to know what they were doing. He pointed to the visitor and said that just two weeks earlier Prince Nakashidze had been sentenced to death for taking part in a plot against the czar.

The titled visitor smilingly admitted that he was a revolutionary and had managed to escape from Russia after the death sentence had been imposed. When he gave his word that he would behave himself and take no part in any political activities against the czar while in Monte Carlo, the wealthy prince was allowed to remain. After that he often appeared at the same parties as his imperial cousins.

The czarina always closed each season by giving a reception for police, at which she presented them with gifts. Unfortunately, these always were the same: bronze watches for the inspectors, silver watches for the commissars and a gold watch and chain for the chief. One inspector who had never been promoted retired with a collection of eighteen imperial bronze watches.

Monaco police also had their hands full with each visit of Leopold II of Belgium. It was not a fear of assassins, but of what the king might do. He had been accused of kidnapping women who caught his fancy. Queen Maria Henrietta, unwilling to witness his steady stream of mistresses, retired to the countryside and let him go on his own. One of the sights at the beach of Cap Ferrat was Leopold carefully draping his beard inside a specially constructed rubber sheath before he entered the water.

Leopold always spoke of himself in the third person, and such instructions to a hotel servant as "Please serve him breakfast at nine o'clock," would leave uninitiated personnel completely baffled, wondering whom they were supposed to serve. Although he was one of the world's wealthiest men —the entire Belgian Congo was his personal private property—he would scrutinize each bill presented to make certain that he was not being overcharged. He demanded sharp creases in everything; even his morning newspapers had to be pressed with a hot iron before they were brought to him on a silver platter.

When he was sixty-five years old, Leopold became enchanted with Caroline Delacroix, an 18-year-old courtesan from the Riviera back hills, who had worked for a time as a waitress. Despite his infatuation, he always treated her like a subordinate; they ate at separate tables in public and never traveled in the same train compartment. Caroline, who was ambitious, wanted him to marry her, but he kept putting her off. The girl resorted to the age-old stratagem of the strip-tease. When they were alone, she would slowly undress in front of him; and when he tried to catch her, she would run away with girlish squeals of laughter, and continue to elude him until the short-winded monarch would sink down exhausted. After a few of these sessions, he gave in and agreed to a morganatic marriage at San Remo. The king's private life had shocked Belgian Cardinal Vaughan, and the prelate publicly had criticized him. In reprisal, Leopold gave Caroline the official title of Baroness Vaughan.

Leopold had two daughters, Stéphanie and Louise. Stéphanie was the wife of Archduke Rudolf at the time of his death at Mayerling. Shortly after they were married, she wrote to a friend about her wedding night: *"Quelle torture, quelle horreur.* I knew nothing. One has led me to the altar like a sacrificial animal. I thought I would die." After the death of her husband, Stéphanie married Count Nagy-Lonyay, at Château Miramar, near Monte Carlo.

Louise, very much against her wishes, was married to an elderly uncle, Prince Philip of Saxe Coburg-Gotha. She lost little time in taking on a procession of lovers. Besides her brother-in-law Rudolf, these included Archduke Louis-Victor and Ferdinand of Bulgaria. Her father did not seem to mind that; but when she fell in love with a man beneath her station, Uhlan Lieutenant Geza Mattachich-Kegelvich, a member of the Hungarian aristocracy, Leopold enlisted the aid of the Austrian Emperor to have her interned in an asylum near Vienna. Mattachich was arrested on a trumped-up charge of falsifying documents and was sentenced to four years in prison. The two lovers managed to escape and fled to Monte Carlo, where they told their story. Louise later was granted a divorce by Prince Philip.

When Leopold died he left 75 million francs to his two daughters, and 135 million to Baroness Vaughan. He also left her the lavish estate Leopolda at Beaulieu. It is now the home of Count Agnelli, head of the Fiat works. The daughters contested the will, and each asked for one quarter of the vast Belgian Congo. Stéphanie was represented in court by Raymond Poincaré, who later became Premier of France. The case dragged on for several years and finally ground to a halt when all the documents were destroyed during the German invasion.

Albert Edward, the Prince of Wales, who was invariably referred to with great affection as "Bertie," had the longest "reign" on the Riviera. From the time he first visited there in 1870 until he became Edward VII in 1901 at the age of fifty-nine, he was the social king of Monte Carlo and rarely missed a season there. In fact, the season was not considered official until he had arrived aboard his yacht, *Britannia*.

Unlike the high-living Russian grand dukes, who put on an ostentatious display and squandered millions at the gaming tables, Bertie preferred to live simply and keep out of the limelight as much as possible. Because his mother Queen Victoria had gone into virtual seclusion following the death of her consort, he had to assume most of the burden of presiding at court ceremonials and public functions, and he sought to relax at the resort and live a private life as Baron Renfrew. The heir to the most important throne in Europe was accompanied by the smallest staff of any visiting member of royalty, just his personal physician and two equerries, and he employed only two menservants and a butler. While he went to the casino almost every night to play baccarat, his wagers were never large enough to call undue public attention to him. Quite often it was his inseparable companion, a fox terrier, who gave away his identity. An inscription on the dog's collar read: *"I am Caesar. I belong to the Prince of Wales."*

Though the prince behaved modestly in public, he was known for his lusty zest for women, food and entertainment, but he was so discreet about many of his romances that Monaco police, who had to keep an eye on all important royal visitors in order to protect the principality from any disaster, frequently, to their great distress, did not know where and with whom he had spent the night.

An ambitious American woman, Mrs. Ogden Goelet, the widow of a multimillionaire, learned to her discomfiture the type of entertainment Bertie preferred. She had wanted to make her mark as one of the leading hostesses on the Riviera and purchased a beautiful château between Cannes and Antibes. After repeated tries she succeeded in having Bertie accept an invitation to dinner at her home, and imprudently asked him if he had any preference for performers for the gala to follow the dinner. He replied that he had never heard Yvette Guilbert sing.

Yvette at that time was well known for singing risqué songs. She was not interested in entertaining at private homes, but Mrs. Goelet bombarded her with telegrams, and the singer set what she thought was an impossible fee, 15,000 francs for two hours of entertainment, roughly $10,000 at that time. Mrs. Goelet, who took the offhand request by the prince as a royal command, promptly wired back accepting the price. The party was the following night.

When Yvette arrived, Mrs. Goelet informed her that the Prince of Wales was the guest of honor and warned her not to sing any off-color songs. The singer complied, and her first two numbers would not have been out of place in a nursery school. Bertie, who had been looking forward to the entertainment, finally called out to her, "Madame, have you come here to sermonize me?"

La Guilbert needed no further encouragement. Disregarding the request of the hostess, she promptly went into her repertoire, each succeeding number saucier than the one before. After a few of these verses, Mrs. Goelet, red-faced, hurried from the salon, soon followed by some of the other women guests. Meanwhile, the Prince of Wales, doubling up with laughter, kept urging the singer on. Yvette's final number was so ribald that she kept her eyes fixed on the ceiling while singing it.

In appreciation for the entertainment, Bertie wrote a letter to the director of London's leading revue theater and suggested that he book the singer. Yvette did appear there later for a six-week stay. Mrs. Goelet sent the singer a check for the agreed fee but without the customary word of thanks. She also never invited Bertie to her home again.

Such actions by the prince were an obvious revolt against the excessive prudishness of his mother's court, but he also was a man of great compassion. While driving in Monte Carlo one day he was hailed by a pedestrian, who doffed his hat in greeting. Bertie did not recognize the man, and he asked his aide if he knew him. The adjutant replied that it was Oscar Wilde, the noted Irish-born poet and playwright.

Wilde had recently been released from Reading Jail, where he had served a two-year sentence following his sensational trial and conviction for sodomy, and he was living in exile in France. The prince promptly ordered the coachman to turn the carriage around, and as he was passing Oscar Wilde, he leaned out and lifted his hat in a wide sweeping bow. It was a spontaneous tribute, not to the author's morals, but to his great literary talents.

Bertie was married to Princess Alexandra, eldest daughter

of Christian IX of Denmark, and she proved to be similarly tolerant. On his very first visit to Monte Carlo in 1870, he was attracted to an American girl, Jane Chamberlayne, of Cleveland, Ohio. She was traveling with her parents, but that did not prevent the prince from pursuing her with dinner invitations. When news of his attention to an American girl reached London, and some of the newspapers even commented about it, Princess Alexandra was annoyed and referred to the girl as "Miss Chamberpots." Actually, his attention in this case was nothing more than a mild flirtation, and the girl returned home with a beautiful diamond necklace as a souvenir. But Princess Alexandra soon became accustomed to her husband's pursuit of women; and with rare understanding, when the king lay dying on the night of May 6, 1910, she saw to it that Mrs. Alice Keppel, his long-time mistress, was brought to his bedside for a final parting. She also arranged for a secret visit to his bier the next day by Lily Langtry, his most famous mistress. Lily said later that Queen Alexandra gave her a beautiful sheaf of roses, which she placed in the king's arms. Lily fondly hoped that he was buried with these roses still in his coffin.

Bertie was a gourmet, and one day while he was dining on the terrace of the Café de Paris, his waiter Henri Carpentier promised to serve him a dessert no one had ever tasted. The waiter prepared a pancake dish to which he added dashes of eau de cerise, curaçao and maraschino. The liqueurs accidentally caught fire on the hot plate, but when Carpentier tasted the slightly burned dish, he was surprised to find that the sample tasted even better than the original he had planned, and so he poured more liqueurs on, kindling flames in various colors.

The prince watched this display with some concern and, at first, sniffed dubiously at the dish when it was set before him, but he smiled happily after his first bite and not only ate every morsel, but also spooned up the remaining liquid. When he asked for the name of the concoction, Carpentier glanced at the young woman seated beside him and suggested that it be called crêpes Princesse.

Bertie winked at his companion, a brunette of undoubted Gallic extraction, and suggested that crêpes Suzette might be a better name.

No one knows the actual identity of Suzette, but her name has become immortal in the history of culinary art. As a result of his accidental fame, Carpentier later came to the United States where he opened his own restaurant.

Bertie's most highly publicized romance was with Lily Langtry; since her flamboyant beauty and personality made her the center of attraction wherever she appeared, it was impossible to keep any association with her a secret.

Lily was born Emily Charlotte Le Breton, the sixth child of William Corbet Le Breton, the Dean of the Isle of Jersey. She was twenty years old when she married Edward Langtry, the wealthy owner of a shipping line, and he brought her to London to introduce her to society. Her great beauty opened many doors, and within a short time she was a member of a select circle and had a procession of lovers, the irrepressible Archduke Rudolf of Austria being among her first. She became such a social celebrity that Oscar Wilde, then twenty-two years old, published a poem in her honor, and vendors sold picture post cards of her on Fleet Street.

The Prince of Wales met her for the first time in June, 1877, at a party in London given by Sir Allen Young. Bertie was fascinated by her beauty and, aware of her reputation, lost little time in going after her; he sent her a note the following morning, announcing that he would call to see her that afternoon. Langtry had to make himself scarce while Bertie and Lily spent several hours together.

From that point on, they were inseparable companions for

the next few years. Later that summer they went together to Monte Carlo, with Langtry ineffectually trailing along for the sake of appearances. Lily sat at the prince's side in the casino, where he gambled with such friends as the Rothschilds and the Sassoons.

Although Bertie is generally credited with being the father of Lily's baby born in 1881, they had drifted somewhat apart by then; Bertie had resumed going out with other women, and Lily was seeing new lovers, including Prince Louis of Battenberg, grandfather of the Duke of Edinburgh, consort of Queen Elizabeth. The Prince of Wales did arrange for Jeanne-Marie's birth in a small nursing home in France. Langtry never saw the baby.

Even though they no longer were lovers, Bertie and Lily remained close friends as long as he lived. As part of his inner circle, she still accompanied him to Monte Carlo even after he became king and made his secret trips there as Baron Renfrew.

Langtry was deeply devoted to his wife despite her scandalous behavior, and he refused all her requests for a divorce. When Langtry suffered business reverses because of her insatiable demand for money, it was Bertie who suggested that she go on the stage and capitalize on the notoriety she had received as his mistress. She followed his advice and toured the United States in 1882, playing to capacity audiences wherever she appeared. This trip was so financially successful that she repeated her American tour for five consecutive seasons and earned several million dollars. In May, 1897, on her last trip, she divorced Langtry in California, charging desertion. He died destitute and in an insane asylum within six months. Two years later she married Sir Hugo Gerald de Bathe, whom she called "Suggie." He was twenty-six, and she was forty-four years old.

One of Lily's greatest stage triumphs resulted from a meeting she had one day in Monte Carlo with a young earl whom she had known as a boy in England. He asked her to accompany him to a fashionable jewelry shop to look at a string of magnificent pearls. She was to pretend to be his sister and simply admire the string.

Lily played along with him and forgot about the incident. She later learned that she had been used as a pawn. The earl, who had run through his fortune, knew the jeweler would recognize Lily and assume the young man was buying the pearls for her. He had no difficulty in obtaining them on credit. He promptly pawned the string for a fraction of its real worth and turned to the gaming tables to recoup his fortune. The result was almost inevitable; he lost the money, and his wealthy relatives had to make good the purchase to prevent his arrest.

Lily employed a ghost writer to turn out a stage comedy, *The Crossways,* based upon this incident. Edward VII gave her a further assist by making the première at the Imperial Theatre in London a royal command performance. The play opened on December 8, 1902, with the king and queen attending.

In one scene Lily had to take the jewels out of a case and admire them. On opening night, instead of following the script, she directed her glance at the royal box, and as she took out each piece of jewelry, she ad-libbed:

"Here is the tiara you gave me in Biarritz, the necklace of diamonds and rubies you fastened around my white throat in Monte Carlo, the rings, the bracelets, the brooches you showered upon me in the glorious past of our flaming passion."

While the audience sat frozen, not knowing what to do, Edward VII—according to Lily's biographer, Ernest Dudley —"chuckled in his beard." He later sent for Lily and congratulated her on her performance, particularly her jewel scene. The word-of-mouth publicity resulting from this incident assured her a sellout not only in England, but later on when she toured the United States with the play.

Lily retired from the stage at the outbreak of World War I and settled in Monte Carlo, where she bought the villa, Le Lys, which overlooks the harbor. Her immediate neighbors were Prince Mirza Reza Khan, in a Persian-style palace; Baroness Orczy, who occupied an Italian-style villa; and Vicente Blasco-Ibáñez, the author of *Four Horsemen of the Apocalypse*.

Her salon was filled with silver-framed photographs of members of royalty who had been her good friends, each containing an exact replica of the appropriate crown. She died in Monte Carlo in 1929.

Bertie's other great love was the English society beauty, Alice Keppel. He met her at Monte Carlo at a party in the villa of the exiled Russian Grand Duke Michael, and largely ceased his philandering after that, content with just this one mistress.

The queens of the night added to the social picture of life at Monte Carlo at this time. With so many members of royalty and millionaires on the loose, it was not surprising that the resort would attract a special kind of demimondaine, elegantly gowned women, sophisticated linguists able to converse in several languages, who behaved in public with decorum. They frequently were indistinguishable from the real ladies present.

Consuelo Vanderbilt found this out to her surprise when she married the Duke of Marlborough and went to Monte Carlo on her wedding trip. She saw several of her husband's friends seated at a table in the dining room of the Hôtel de Paris in the company of three beautiful women, each one a perfect picture of propriety. The American bride was ready to go over with greetings when the duke skillfully steered her away and explained that ladies did not meet socially with that kind of woman.

It was only those who used lipstick, then frowned upon by respectable society, who drew a recognizable cherry-red line in external appearances between the two worlds.

During the Victorian era these two worlds were kept completely separate. The cocottes had their own code: they never tried to make the acquaintance of their benefactors' families, nor did they attempt to mingle, outside of business, in polite society. Few ladies at that time did more than go sightseeing briefly at the casino, and so the field was left open for the prostitutes, particularly after midnight when the last train had left.

There were no gambling casinos in France then, and wealthy guests would come from Cannes and Nice. Many sent their servants ahead with a wardrobe, and they retained suites in hotels where they could change clothes or rest from the railroad journey. Quite often the men would be busy at the tables when the last train was ready to leave, and they would send their wives back home while they remained on to play. The play often included the waiting courtesans.

Jean Cocteau, who liked to watch these women in action, kept a diary in which he wrote this observation:

"Saw Otero and Cavalieri at supper tonight. That was no small affair. Nothing but casings, sheaths, whalebones, silkcords, shoulderstraps, leggings, cuisses, gantlets, corselets, pearl halters, feather bucklers, coats of mail, velvet and satin belts.

"These knights bristling with gems, tulle and eyelashes, these sacred beetles armed with asparagus pincers, these Samurais in sable and ermine, these cuirassiers of pleasure whom robust soubrettes had harnessed and caparisoned since dawn, seemed as little able to get out of their armor as an oyster out of its shell.

"Undressing one of these ladies obviously was a costly enterprise that had to be prepared in advance, like moving a household."

It was significant that Cocteau mentioned Otero by name. She was indeed the queen of them all. A golden-skinned gypsy from Andalusia with a magnificent figure, she slept in more royal beds than any other woman in Europe. Edward VII sent her the shortest invitation on record; it was simply a clock dial, drawn on a piece of paper, showing the time she was to appear.

She preferred to wear simple black evening gowns adorned only by two rows of pearls. When one of her rivals, in a bid for attention, came to the casino one night bedecked with dozens of glittering jewels, Otero paid her back in kind. She marched through the *salons privés* the next night wearing only a black gown, not even her pearls. But directly behind her was her maid, a robust Swiss woman, who sparkled like a Christmas tree, completely covered from head to foot with Otero's jewels.

Caroline Otero was fourteen years old when she appeared in Monte Carlo the first time, the child bride of an Italian baron. According to legend, her husband had lost his money playing roulette. All he had left was ten louis d'or, which he gave to her. She went inside the salon and dropped the money on the green baize. The croupier raked up the little gold heap, and Caroline started watching her neighbors. As the minutes went by, excitement gripped those in the salon, and they converged at her table, whispering and staring at her. The young girl was embarrassed by so much attention. Suddenly one of the men standing near her pointed to a huge pile of chips and begged her to pick them up.

She had placed her ten louis on red, and when she saw the croupier rake in the gold pieces, she thought she had lost; he was replacing them with chips. Meanwhile, red had come

up twenty-one times in a row, and her winnings had totaled
$30,000. She had not gambled before and knew nothing about
playing roulette.

Whether this is true or not, she later became one of the
heaviest plungers in the history of the casino. Born near Se-
ville, the little gypsy had left home to conquer the world
with her voice, her guitar and castanets, and she did conquer
an important segment of it with her body. Kings, princes,
bankers and millionaires of all kinds and nationalities vied
with each other for her attention.

The Government of France, which took a practical view
of such matters, placed Otero at the head of the list of special services that the Elysée and the Quai d'Orsay offered
royal visitors. Since it was difficult to fit such moments of lei-
sure into official programs of receptions, gala performances
and military inspections, Otero was always scheduled under
the heading, "Visit to the President of the Senate." No one
could quite figure out the functions of the office of the President of the Senate in the Third Republic, but it did serve as
an excellent cover in entertaining royal guests.

All of this added to Otero's fees at Monte Carlo, and these
were set according to her idea of the ugliness of the man.
The ugliest man she ever encountered was a German baron,
Theo Ollstreder. She met him while starring in a pantomime
in the Berlin Wintergarten that reputedly had been written
by Kaiser Wilhelm II. Although she could have had her pick
of dukes and princes, she selected Ollstreder because he was
the richest of them all. He followed her to Monte Carlo,
and every evening sent her his visiting card to which he had
thoughtfully attached a costly jewel. Otero was heard to say,
"At that rate no man really can be called ugly."

After she toured the United States, Frank Juergens, an
American impresario, embezzled $50,000 to follow her to
Monte Carlo. The explorer Jean Payen killed himself be-

cause she had rejected him, and Count Cheney, a member
of the Jockey Club, shot himself when he lost two million
francs at the casino trying to curry her favor. American newspapers referred to her as the "Suicide Siren."

After a tour of Russia, where many grand dukes had
played host to her, she returned with a jewel collection that
included necklaces that once had belonged to Empress Eu-
génie of France, Empress Elizabeth of Austria and Marie
Antoinette, plus assorted baubles such as a pair of earrings,
each one of which contained fifty carats of diamonds.

But Monte Carlo, which had started Otero on her career,
collected heavy interest for it. She retired in 1922 at the age
of forty-five with an estimated fortune of 10 million dollars
in jewels, furs and paintings. Within a few years she had lost
everything at the gaming tables. Caroline Otero, now eighty-
six, lives in a narrow room in the Rue d'Angleterre in Nice
on a small pension paid to her by the casino.

Other noted courtesans were Émilienne d'Alençon, a mistress of Leopold II, who would write letters to her in printed
characters in an attempt to disguise his handwriting; Liane
de Pougy, whose favorite jeweler followed her around with a
large selection of his stock in case a client wanted to buy her
favors; and Juniory, a tall, willowy blonde, who was courted
by ten different millionaires in succession. Juniory was passionately fond of horses and carriages and had the finest on
the Riviera. Her bed was a replica of a large pink seashell
held up by four silver Neptunes.

De Pougy, who lost out to Otero as the ruling queen, received a last-moment invitation from librettist Henri Meilhac to accompany him to a presentation of his opera *Manon*
in Monte Carlo. When she entered the box, she was surprised to see the audience stand while the orchestra played
a stirring tune. She asked Meilhac what was going on. "Oh,
the Queen of Sweden was supposed to be here but she didn't

feel well." He stared blandly down at the audience and added, "I didn't notify the management or the orchestra of the change."

She later married Prince Ghika of Rumania. When they were divorced after twenty-seven years of marriage, she took the vows, entered a Lausanne convent and died there in 1942.

The Edwardian era in Monte Carlo was responsible for a change in society's attitude toward these women; they were accepted if they made a successful marriage. Hall porters at the Hôtel de Paris still tell about the meeting of two women in a narrow passageway, with each refusing to give precedence to the other.

"Madam," one of them said, "I am a princess."

"That's because your mother was luckier than mine," the other replied. "My father, the King, did not marry her."

The second speaker was the beautiful Bianca, who publicly proclaimed that she was an illegitimate daughter of Edward VII, born when he was the Prince of Wales.

Although World War I toppled many monarchies, Monte Carlo still plays host to some of the remaining members of royalty. Bertie's grandson, the present Duke of Windsor, was a constant visitor while he was Prince of Wales, and since his abdication he spends a part of each season on the Riviera with his wife, the former Wallis Simpson. King Farouk was a noted bettor before he lost his throne, and he still is one of the biggest gamblers in the casino.

One of the most unusual gamblers among the royal visitors was the Prince of Nepal, whose revenue was estimated at $20,000 a day. The Monte Carlo jewelers were particularly happy to see him since he collected gems like other people buy postage stamps. He owned a diamond necklace that was three yards long, which some wit dubbed "the Ganges of the Colliers."

The prince's religion did not allow him to gamble except

for five days a year, and during these five days and nights, he rarely ate, drank or slept, spending all his time in the *salons privés*. The casino was kept open for him for as long as he wanted to play. Although he never entered the casino carrying any money, it did not matter. He was the only client croupiers had orders to keep supplied with stacks of 1,000-franc chips at all times. When the five days were up, he promptly stopped gambling for the year and settled his debts.

A few years ago Monaco police ran into a nasty situation involving an Eastern potentate. The body of an 18-year-old blonde, who had worked in a florist shop near the casino, was found in the bay of Monte Carlo. Clasped between her fingers was a note reading, "They wanted to take me to the harem of ———. I prefer to die." The name given on the note was that of an Arabian prince.

When detectives interviewed the prince, he said he had never seen nor heard of the girl, and insisted that an enemy must be plotting against him. He said he had recently quarreled with the potentate over a gambling debt. Some of the facts developed by the investigation tended to support the prince's story. The coroner said the note had been placed between the girl's fingers after her death. The girl's body was covered with bruises, indicating that she had been flogged.

Police began a quiet investigation of the potentate, and they soon learned that his aides were busy scanning the Riviera for pretty girls, between sixteen and eighteen years old, and luring them to his yacht, where they were mistreated by the ruler. The girls had been too frightened to complain later to police. When he learned that he was under investigation in the death of the florist girl, his yacht sailed immediately. There was no pursuit since he had diplomatic immunity, but he knows he cannot return to Monaco.

Some members of genuine royalty now living in Monte Carlo are too poor to play at the casino. Prince Nicolas of

Greece, the father of the Duchess of Kent, did not go to his daughter's wedding because he said he did not have the money to pay the fare. However, the casino no longer is concerned about the dearth of royalty. The new king today is the tourist from all over the world, and though the individual bets may be small, they add up to a satisfying total when the books are balanced at the end of each year.

CHAPTER 3

Monaco's First American Princess

For all the journalistic hubbub that surrounded the marriage of screen actress Grace Kelly to Prince Rainier, and despite the continuing stream of words that still appears yearly in print, keeping alive the fairy-tale aspects of an American commoner wed to a reigning prince, even the most diligent of readers would be hard pressed to find any mention of the fact that Princess Grace is not the first American woman to share the throne of Monaco.

The forgotten American princess, who also was a beautiful blonde, was Alice Heine, a member of the famous banking family, a grandniece of the noted poet, Heinrich Heine; and at her death in 1925, the Dowager Princess of Monaco. It is strange that she should be overlooked since it was largely due to the efforts of Princess Alice that Monte Carlo was converted from little more than a gambling casino, shunned then by most respectable women, into one of the cultural centers of the world. She was the moving force behind the Monte Carlo opera, theater and ballet. She prodded great performers into coming there, encouraged composers to experiment and forced the casino to support these artistic en-

deavors, which, in a short time, became one of its greatest
drawing cards, attracting even nongamblers to the resort.

Although her family had drifted away from Judaism, and
she was a Catholic, the same inner conflicts which had disturbed Heinrich Heine during much of his life also were
present within her. With her husband, Prince Albert, she took
an active part in fighting for a new trial for Captain Alfred
Dreyfus in the anti-Semitic scandal that rocked France, and
she helped establish a Monacan tradition, which still exists,
of a lack of religious bias in the principality. Prince Louis,
Rainier's grandfather, saved the lives of hundreds of Jews
who were trapped in Monte Carlo during its occupation by
the Nazis.

Unlike Princess Grace, though, Alice Heine's life was
tinged with a number of scandals that made her one of
Europe's most talked-about socially prominent women.

The future princess was born February 10, 1858, at 902
Royal Street, in the Vieux Carré district of New Orleans.
The address is a city landmark, the Miltenberger House. This
beautiful mansion with its lacy ironwork, first constructed in
1838, is one of the tourist sights in New Orleans and is featured on souvenir picture post cards of the city. These cards
make no mention of Alice Heine.

She was the daughter of Michael Heine and Marie Miltenberger. Her father, a grandson of Solomon Heine, the
famous Hamburg banker, had been sent to the United States
to open a branch of the family bank. He settled in New
Orleans, shipping headquarters for the South's cotton, and
married Miss Miltenberger, a member of a family socially
prominent in the city since the early 1700's.

Heinrich Heine mentioned in his fragmentary memoirs
that his grandmother, whom he described as resembling "the
abbess of a Protestant convent," had been a very beautiful and
distinguished-looking woman. "Of her children," he wrote,

"only my father and my uncle, Solomon, inherited her good looks. Solomon's children without exception grew up to be charmingly beautiful, but death took them in their bloom, and only two are left. I loved all of them dearly."

The family good looks, of which Heinrich Heine boasted, evidently passed on to Alice. She was sixteen years old, slender, with exceptionally large blue eyes, when her father brought her to Paris. The New Orleans beauty seems to have exploded into French society like a bombshell.

The banking branch of the Heine family, like their rivals, the Rothschilds, had spread their activities to many cities of Europe. Michael's widowed mother, who was a Furtado, a wealthy French Jewish banking family, had returned to Paris. His brother Armand was head of the Furtado-Heine banking house in France, and his young sister Paule was married to the Duke of Elchingen, a grandson of Marshal Ney, Napoleon's great general.

Paule, the Duchess of Elchingen, took on the task of introducing her pretty niece to French society, and held balls in her honor at both her town house on Rue Jean Goujon, just off the Champs-Élysées, and at their palace near Paris, the Château de Rocquencourt.

The fresh beauty of the visiting belle from New Orleans captivated French society, and despite her youth, there was an immediate rush of suitors. Arthur Mayer, who was the leading social reporter of that time, wrote that she was "lovely like a Tanagra figure," comparing her to the exquisite figurines that had been discovered in the ancient Greek city.

It was at the château that Alice was introduced to Duke Armand de Richelieu, titular head of one of France's most eminent families and important titles, and one of the most eligible bachelors in Europe. In true fairy-tale fashion, the duke, then twenty-six years old, fell deeply in love with the American girl and proposed to her a short time later.

The French aristocrat and the American teen-ager were married in Paris on February 27, 1875, some two weeks after Alice's seventeenth birthday. That same year, on December 21, Alice also became a mother and the elated Duke announced the birth of an heir. The boy was baptized Marie Odéon Jean Armand de Chapelle de Juilhac de Richelieu. The young couple remained happily married, and Alice, an extrovert with a bubbling, effervescent personality, quickly established herself as one of the leading hostesses in France. She not only accepted the traditional role of Lady Bountiful to the peasants living near the Château de Haut-Buisson, but she broadened her charitable activities and also took a lively interest in the arts and in politics. Many noted figures of the day were invited to her salon. Even though Monte Carlo was becoming popular with the titled rich, the couple showed no interest in the resort. Four years after the marriage a daughter, Odile, was born at Haut-Buisson. The following year the Duke of Richelieu became ill while in Athens, and he was only thirty-two when he died on June 28, 1880.

With the successful marriage of his daughter, Michael Heine severed his connections in the United States, moved permanently to France and joined his brother in the banking firm, which was renamed Heine Frères. When Armand's daughter Odile married Achille Fould, that family's bank was brought into the business. Later the brothers helped found the Banque d'Union Parisienne, which is still one of the leading financial institutions in France.

One of Michael Heine's personal clients was his daughter's friend, Sarah Bernhardt. The actress, delighted with the way the banker was shrewdly building up her fortune, would refer to him fondly as her "golden pig."

The vivacious Alice, who was only twenty-two years old when the duke died, soon showed signs that she had no intentions of donning widow's weeds for any prolonged period, and her worried family induced her to go away for a rest, thoughtfully selecting Madeira, a small volcanic Portuguese island well off the coast of Africa, where they hoped she would have little to do but be soothed by the healthful climate and the monotonous splashing of waves on the shore. The announcement was made that she was going there because of her delicate health, indicating to the public that she was ravaged by her recent bereavement.

Disquieting news, however, was soon received from Funchal, the capital city of Madeira, where Alice had settled. She was seeing a doctor, but his visits were neither professional nor platonic; she had fallen in love with the doctor, and he was Jewish.

Michael Heine, who liked to refer to his daughter as the Duchess de Richelieu, hurried to the far-off island and succeeded in ending the romance. He brought Alice to Biarritz to finish her recuperation. The same pattern repeated itself there; once again her constant companion was a doctor, and once again he was Jewish. There was little the family could do; not only was Alice of age, but she had inherited a sizable fortune from her husband, almost 15 million dollars, quite enough to be independent. But this romance needed no interference; it came to its own end, and Alice returned to her château.

The duchess resumed entertaining and divided her time between Haut-Buisson and a Paris town house in Faubourg St-Honoré, and her salon here became noted for the stimulating parties she gave where members of the upper class mingled with the leading politicians, writers and artists of the day.

One of Alice's neighbors in Paris was Prince Albert of Monaco, heir to the throne, who had his own town house almost next door. The duchess and the prince had met briefly during her stay at Funchal, where he had headed a scientific expedition to conduct deep-sea diving experiments in the waters around Madeira; he was an ardent and world-recognized oceanographer. Alice invited her neighbor to one of her receptions, and the prince was fascinated by both her beauty and her vibrant personality; they began going out together.

Albert was a divorced man. He had been married to Lady Mary-Victoria Douglas Hamilton, daughter of the Scottish Duke of Hamilton. Her mother was Princess Marie of Baden.

The marriage of the prince, then twenty, and Lady Hamilton, eighteen years old, had been arranged by Napoleon III; there was no love on either side. Society was startled some five months later when the new princess, although pregnant, left her husband and returned home to her mother. Gossips reported that Prince Albert had struck her when she objected to his constant running around with women; he was as notorious on the Riviera for his many love affairs as Bertie the Prince of Wales, and Leopold II. Others claimed her leaving was due to the intrigues of Monsignor Theurat, Bishop of Monaco, who did not like Lady Hamilton. The runaway wife later gave birth to Albert's son, Louis Honoré Charles Antoine, Prince Rainier's grandfather, at Baden-Baden.

Some five years after she had walked out on Albert, an attempt was made to patch up the marriage, but the princess, who had resumed calling herself Lady Hamilton, refused to see him again. A Church annulment was granted, and the civil marriage was legally dissolved by divorce. The handsome dowry she had brought remained firmly in the Grimaldi treasury. Lady Hamilton later married an Hungarian count.

Prince Albert was very much in love with Alice and wanted to marry her, but his father, reigning Prince Charles III, refused to grant permission. He had seen his son's first marriage blow up, and he feared that Albert and the duchess were not temperamentally suited to each other. Albert was a quiet, introspective, almost taciturn man, interested mainly in his scientific projects. Psychologists say that his scandalous romances during his youth were an attempt to compensate for his almost painful shyness. Alice, on the other hand, was an extrovert, full of American drive and nervous energy, a brilliant wit and an almost compulsive talker. She quickly became excited and enthusiastic about projects and would immediately plunge into them.

Whether the couple became lovers not long after they met, or whether Alice finally became Albert's mistress only after his father had refused to sanction the marriage is their own secret, but their romance was openly discussed. Further to confound the father, the affair continued for some years without a break, and one month after Prince Charles died, on October 30, 1889, they were married in Paris, the civil portion in the mayor's office of the Eighth Arrondissement, and the religious ceremony in the Chapel of the Nunciatura in the Rue de Varenne.

The newlyweds made their triumphal entry into Monte Carlo on January 13, 1890, cheered by the watching population, and were received by Msg. Theurat on the threshold of the cathedral—where Grace Kelly was married sixty-six years later. In his welcoming address, the Bishop of Monaco said to Alice:

"And you, Princess, who are a Christian woman par excellence, you who are the embodiment of virtue, charity and generosity, come and take your place at the side of him who, after having appreciated you so well, presents you today, at the start of his reign, as a gift to the Principality."

Princess Alice brought more than a well-filled purse. Her boundless energy soon revitalized the once sleepy court. François de Bernardy, an historian of the principality, wrote, "The marriage started under the happiest auspices. The princess was as intelligent as she was pretty. Her blonde beauty lit up the palace that had been sad for so many years, and shook it out of its long lethargy. A perfect hostess, the Duchess of Richelieu had held a brilliant salon in Paris. Now the Princess of Monaco attracted the world of the arts and the theater to the Rock and to the new Opera of Monte Carlo."

Actually, Princess Alice had been horrified at her first sight of compulsive gamblers in the casino and urged her husband to close down the place, but she quickly changed her mind when Prince Albert pointed out that the economy of the principality was based on the casino, particularly the two million gold francs that were stacked so shiny bright in the Grimaldi treasury.

The reports of her displeasure worried casino officials. The original 50-year lease still had some years to run, but Camille Blanc, the director, wanted to insure its continuance, and his emissaries hurried to the palace and suggested an extension. Aware now of the casino's importance, Alice stifled her objections, and swiftly seized upon the request as a lever to make Monte Carlo an important cultural center, attractive to women. It was freely admitted that Princess Alice was the guiding spirit behind the negotiations that led to a new 50-year concession, and she proved herself to be a true member of the Heine banking family, able to drive a hard and shrewd bargain.

The settlement included the immediate payment of 10 million francs into the state treasury and an additional payment of 50 million francs to be made in 1914, when the original concession was to expire. The casino further agreed to spend not less than two million francs to construct an opera house as part of the building and to contribute 25,000 francs for each of twenty-four performances a season. In addition, the casino was to pay to the Grimaldis a further royalty of 5 per cent of its receipts whenever it went over 25 million francs a year. And since the casino was profitable, practical

Alice saw to it that Prince Albert was to be allowed to purchase 1,000 shares of stock in the owning company. By the
end of the third year of their marriage he had increased his
holdings to 1,400 shares. Since Alice always was a strong supporter of the needy, the agreement further provided that the
casino had to contribute an immediate five million francs to
local charities. Monégasques had reason to be pleased with
their new princess, and an English woman observer at the
scene wrote, "So kind and charming was she that 'the Princess
Alice' soon became the idol of the people, perhaps the most
popular princess Monaco had ever owned."

Prince Albert shared his wife's interest in the theater. He
was fond of recalling that his grandfather Prince Florestan
had been an actor in Paris when the Grimaldis were temporarily toppled off their throne during the French Revolution. In 1892, when the opera house was completed, Raoul
Gunsbourg, famous as an impresario in France and Russia,
was appointed director of the Monte Carlo Opera House, and
he soon made it one of the outstanding ones in Europe. He
was the first to stage the operas of Wagner outside of Bay-
reuth, helped popularize the works of Massenet and also
brought the best plays of the Comédie Française to the theater.
He discovered Diaghilev and his ballet, and provided a permanent place for him at Monte Carlo. He worked in closest
co-operation with Princess Alice, and she used her best per-
suasive talents to bring all the great actors, singers, composers
and conductors to the opera house. With Alice's spirited
encouragement, new great ballets and musical compositions
that have enriched the world were first performed at Monte
Carlo. Gunsbourg was to remain for fifty years until his retirement after World War II. He celebrated his one hun-
dredth birthday in 1961 and, at this writing, is still alive.

Alice failed to share one enthusiasm with Prince Albert,
his love for oceanography. Although he named his two suc-

cessive and expensively equipped yachts after her, the 600-ton *Alice* and the 1,400-ton *Alice II,* she never even boarded them. She was a poor sailor and would get seasick even on a ship anchored in a glassy-still harbor. Prince Albert frequently left on scientific expeditions.

The couple were strongly united, though, in the Dreyfus affair. Captain Dreyfus, a Jewish artillery officer on the French general staff, was arrested in 1894 and accused of being the author of an anonymous letter that gave away important military information to the German military attaché at Paris. Although there was no credible evidence against Dreyfus, the information contained in the letter unquestionably had come from a member of the general staff. Since the appointment of a Jew had not been popular with his colleagues, Dreyfus was made the scapegoat, was convicted of treason at a secret court-martial, condemned to public degradation at a military ceremony and sentenced to life imprisonment on Devil's Island. Immediately afterward, a well-prepared propaganda campaign against Jews broke out in France, but it had been organized too well; many people became suspicious, and there were sharp divisions throughout the country over the innocence or guilt of Captain Dreyfus.

Two years later Colonel Georges Picquart, head of intelligence for the French War Office, uncovered information clearing Dreyfus and implicating Major Esterhazy, one of the chief witnesses against Dreyfus, as the actual writer of the letter. The general staff promptly sent Picquart on a dangerous mission to Tunisia and moved Lieutenant Colonel Henry into his place as head of intelligence. But information about Picquart's findings leaked out, and agitation for Dreyfus' release continued. In an attempt to still the clamor, the War Office went through the motions of placing Esterhazy on trial, and he was promptly acquitted at his court-martial.

But public indignation could not be stilled, and prominent intellectuals and leading Liberals and Socialists, including Georges Clemenceau and Anatole France, fought for a revision of the Dreyfus verdict. Émile Zola wrote his stirring open letter, *"J'Accuse,"* and had to flee to England to avoid jail. France was close to civil war over the Dreyfus case when the Army, in a desperate effort, presented to the Chamber of Deputies what it claimed was documentary proof of Dreyfus' guilt. Six weeks later Lieutenant Colonel Henry admitted he had forged the documents, and committed suicide. The continuing scandal forced a paper shuffling of the general staff and the dismissal of Esterhazy, but the Army still loudly insisted that Dreyfus was guilty. Esterhazy went to England, where he confessed his guilt. The Court of Cassation, the highest court of appeal in France, finally ordered a new trial.

While all this was going on, Princess Alice was an ardent supporter of Captain Dreyfus. As the Duchess of Richelieu, she had entertained in her famous Paris salon many of the important political figures and intellectuals who were leading the fight for Dreyfus. Even before the new trial was ordered, and possibly at Alice's request, Prince Albert, who was a personal friend of Kaiser Wilhelm II, went to Berlin. The kaiser, who was in a position to know, told Prince Albert that Dreyfus was innocent, and gave him permission to transmit that message to French President Félix Faure. Prince Albert saw President Faure on February 16, 1899, at 5 P.M., and remained with him for twenty minutes. Faure, who had been against any revision of the trial, suffered a stroke within a half-hour after receiving the information from Prince Albert.

When the new trial was ordered, Prince Albert injected himself further into the case when he made public this letter he had sent to Mme. Dreyfus:

You have defended the honor of your husband with
admirable valiance, and impartial justice is getting
ready to grant you a long overdue reparation.

To help all honest people to make you forget so many
pains and sufferings, I herewith invite you and your husband to come and visit me at the Château de Marchais as
soon as the sacred work of Justice has been accomplished.

The presence of a martyr, toward whom the conscience
of humanity turns with anxiety, will honor my house.

Among the sympathies which are going toward you,
Madame, there can be no more sincere nor more respect-
ful ones than mine.

                              Albert, Prince of Monaco

The release of this letter caused a sensation in France,
where the Army was fighting a last-ditch battle against Dreyfus. Since Prince Albert had shown little interest in government affairs of his own principality, let alone that of a neighboring country, the finger was pointed at Princess Alice as
being behind his letter, and Count Boni de Castellane, the
husband of American heiress Anna Gould, who was a French
senator and a leading defender of the Army, made a barely
disguised anti-Semitic attack against her when he wrote in
an intemperate letter to Prince Albert: "Perhaps, Monsei-
gneur, you are a relative by alliance of Captain Dreyfus, but
in that case it is premature for you to triumph." His phrase,
"a relative by alliance of Captain Dreyfus," was, of course,
a reference to the Jewish ancestry of Princess Alice.

His letter also said: "You meddle into a matter that
is none of your business, Your Most Serene Highness. If you
think you can influence French officers in the grave deci-
sion they will take, I beg of you to remember that the game
is not equal, for none of us would ask the permission of a
prince in tutelage," the latter a pointed reference to France's

A study in contrasts—above, the city and fortress of Monaco at the end of the 17th century *(Photo Viollet)*. Below, a bird's-eye view of Monaco, 1962 *(Photo Detaille)*.

The blind Prince Charles III of Monaco, for whom Monte Carlo is named.

François Blanc, the fifth concessionaire the casino, who started it on its brillia career *(Photo Detaille).*

Camille Blanc, François' son and successor *(Photo Detaille).*

Camille Blanc, in foreground, with Ra Gunsbourg, director of the Monte Ca Opera, left, and Enrico Caruso.

Prince Albert, husband of Alice
Heine, first American princess of
Monaco.

Princess Alice of Monaco (*Photo
Detaille*).

Monte Carlo, 1907-08—above, the **Café de Paris** *(Collection Viollet).*
Below, inside the casino, Salle Schmidt *(Photo Viollet).*

strong hold over Monaco, of which Prince Rainier has since become very much aware.

Few people are aware that the Army still would not admit any part in the plot and that Dreyfus again was found guilty at his retrial, but the officers hoped to appease public wrath by imposing only a 10-year sentence. This was too much for the Government, which stepped in directly and issued a full pardon. It was not until six years later, when the Court of Cassation again reviewed the case, that the court-martial was nullified, and the evidence against Dreyfus officially branded a forgery. He was finally reinstated in the Army with the rank of major.

The same year that Count de Castellane cast his barbs at Princess Alice, she also was on the receiving end of a strong rebuff from Queen Victoria of England. The queen, who had started out merely disliking Monte Carlo for its sinful ways, had come to loathe it because it was the favorite playground of her son Bertie, the Prince of Wales, and his antics there every season provided scandal newspapers with an unending source of material. Prince Albert and Princess Alice were Bertie's personal friends. And Queen Victoria was not unaware of the gossip that had preceded their marriage.

While Queen Victoria was wintering at the Hotel Regina Palace in Nice, she received a message that Prince Albert wanted to pay her a courtesy visit with his wife. The queen sent word that she would be busy until Easter, and that he might ask again after the holidays, a most polite but firm royal brushoff. For some inexplicable reason, Prince Albert refused to recognize the obvious, and he renewed his request after Easter. This time Queen Victoria removed the velvet glove. Although she could not readily refuse to see a reigning prince, she did not have to receive his wife, and she made this pointedly clear by sending a letter that read: "Her Majesty will have the honor to receive His Serene Highness,

the Prince of Monaco." No mention was made in the letter of
Princess Alice. There was little courtesy in that courtesy
visit.

As Prince Charles had shrewdly foreseen, the strongly
divergent personalities of Prince Albert and Princess Alice
slowly began to erode their marriage. Albert had considered
the opera house of joint interest to them, but Alice took over
more and more. She dominated the theater, made many de-
cisions without consulting him, and he was angry when he
learned that she had authorized the spending of 200,000
francs in production costs for a one-night opera performance.
He said she was a wastrel and seemed to suffer from *"folie
de grandeur."*

Prince Albert started his deep-sea museum at Monte
Carlo and left on more frequent scientific cruises to the
Azores or the west coast of Africa, and these began to last
longer, months at a time. Alice still was a vigorous woman
in her late thirties, and she was bored with palace life outside the season, so she also began spending more time away
from Monaco, in Paris or on trips to other countries. Occasionally she would leave shortly before Albert was due back
from a cruise, and then return only after he had sailed again.

Another source of difficulty between them was her spon-
sorship of a young British composer, Isidore de Lara, who
had changed his name from Cohen. He had been a drawing-
room idol of London society, where he would sing his own
songs, and was the author of a hit song of that era entitled,
"Garden of Sleep."

With her well known enthusiasm, Princess Alice took him
under her wing and induced Gunsbourg to allow him to
stage such operas as *Carmen* and *Otello* at Monte Carlo.
With Prince Albert away on his trips now even during the
season, de Lara frequently accompanied her to the performances. She pushed the musician into writing operas of his

own, and it was on the production of his *Messalina* that she
had spent the 200,000 francs.

On her recommendation, Gunsbourg personally staged
de Lara's opera, *Amy Rossart.* The première took place in
the presence of Her Serene Highness, while Albert was off
on still another cruise. The opera was a success, but Monégasques were becoming uneasy about her constant compan-
ionship with the musician, and it was creating talk. During that night somebody scrawled a message in chalk on the
palace walls. It read: *"Ici dort de Lara."* ("Here sleeps de
Lara.") Prince Albert was not amused when he returned
from his cruise and learned about the episode. The couple
had a bitter quarrel, and not long afterward some of the
more sensational newspapers published cautious hints that
the marriage was in difficulty. When there was no vigorous
denial from the palace, they nibbled further at the story,
some of the papers hinting that the prince would sue for
divorce and name an English musician. Alice did leave the
palace, and in May, 1902, an official separation was obtained,
but there was no divorce. Alice remained Her Serene Highness, Princess of Monaco, until the death of Albert, and then
became the Dowager Princess.

Shortly before the final breakup, Prince Albert was returning on a train from Potsdam, and he discussed American women with Loie Fuller, a dancer from the United
States. Though he was speaking generally, he may have revealed more about his life with Alice than he realized when
he said:

"You American women are too new. You leave too little
room for the lords of creation. How can we hold our own if
you make inroads upon the intellectual domain which has
always been sacred to us? Exceptions like Sappho only prove
the rule. Your society women ride astride. They are too
much in the newspapers. I prefer the old rule of a woman

appearing only three times in the press, at birth, at her marriage and at her death. Your women are cold sepulchers, they have too much head power. They may be statuesque, but masterful women are an abomination."

His princess was an American woman, an intellectual with "head power," as he phrased it; her figure was statuesque, particularly as she matured; and she was a determined woman who wanted to run things her way, particularly the Monte Carlo Opera.

Alice was forty-four years old when she was separated from Prince Albert, and she lost little time in resuming her life as a leading hostess, but this time she substituted London for Paris. She spent half her time at Haut-Buisson and the remainder of the year in her apartment at Claridge's in London, which she maintained year-round. De Lara was her frequent companion, giving gossips additional ammunition. She was a close personal friend of Queen Alexandra, Bertie's wife (he was now Edward VII), and the queen made up for the rebuff by Victoria by presenting Alice with a special variety of rose grown only at Windsor Castle. Alice planted it at Haut-Buisson, and during her lifetime these roses were grown only at these two places.

As in France, her apartment in England became a gathering place for members of society, politicians and creative artists. She was privy to many important events, since the head power that Prince Albert had complained about was recognized in both France and England, and her advice was sought. Winston Churchill enjoyed visits to her salon. Her views were described as always very liberal, cosmopolitan and sophisticated.

She poured a fortune into transforming Haut-Buisson into one of the most luxurious homes in France and, since she always was an innovator, equipped it with all the modern devices she could find. She employed the finest chefs, and her invitations were eagerly sought after. Titled Englishmen frequently crossed the Channel simply to be her dinner guests.

She also was known for her caustic wit. A very wealthy American woman, trying to crash Paris society, sent invitations to a most select group, who turned up out of curiosity. Princess Alice was one of them. As they were leaving, she turned to a friend and remarked, "This was really a very nice party. Everyone knew everyone else." She paused and then added, "It's too bad nobody got to know the hostess."

At the outbreak of World War I, Alice was in England and remained there for the duration. She supported a hospital in France and largely underwrote the French Hospital in England, and she became a one-person canteen, bringing under her wing the wives of all French soldiers stranded in England. After the war the French Government presented her with the Medal of French Gratitude. Among other decorations, she received the Gold Medal of the Italian Red Cross.

Alice did not forget that she was American-born. When President Woodrow Wilson came to France for the Versailles Peace Conference, she no longer had a town house in Paris, but her cousin, Duchess Cécile d'Elchingen, had a beautiful home at 20, Rue Monceau. With her typical energy, she moved her cousin out, and the house was placed at President Wilson's disposal. He lived there for several months.

In late December, 1925, she left Haut-Buisson planning to spend the Christmas holidays in England. While en route she was stricken with a heart attack and taken to a Paris hotel, where she died on December 23, at the age of sixty-eight. A requiem mass was held for her three days later in the Madeleine Church in Paris. The first two pages of the *Journal of Monaco*, the official bulletin of the principality, were devoted just to listing the names of the more than five hundred persons who had attended the services. Members from most of the great families of France were present. All the Grimaldis came, including Albert's son, the reigning Prince Louis II of Monaco.

Alice's own family made an impressive list of titles. These included her son, the Duke de Richelieu; her daughter and son-in-law, Count and Countess Gabriel de La Rochefoucauld; George Heine, Regent of the Bank of France; and such cousins as the Prince de la Moskawa, the Duke d'Elchingen, the Prince d'Essling, the Duke d'Albufera and the Duke de Fezensac. French statesmen included such personal friends as André Tardieu and Jules Cambon. The court paper also listed M. Isidore de Lara.

On January 4, 1926, a similar mass was held in London at the Church of Immaculate Conception, attended by many members of British nobility.

Within days of her death, extraordinary tributes to her appeared in both London and France. The London *Times* published a letter that praised Princess Alice for her beauty, charm, wit and her many charitable works. The *Eclaireur de Nice* ran a lengthy editorial entitled, "Death of a Good Fairy," and used such encomia as "svelte, scintillant blonde beauty, graceful, clear voice, gleaming eyes, infectious laughter."

"The official title of Serenissime poorly fitted this soul of fire," the editorial went on. "She was of a great sensibility, moved by all suffering and enthused by all noble dreams. She conceived charity as a passion. She was the good-hearted servant of the underprivileged, but didn't like that to be talked about. She gave and gave." The same editorial said: "She knew thoroughly the English, French and Italian literatures and could talk with equal authority about Tuscan primitives, Venetian masters and Byzantine or Roman art.

She was very proud of counting Heinrich Heine among her ancestors. She possessed admirable frankness, a superior disdain of all hypocrisy, an indulgence for all human weaknesses, but was intransigent about lies."

Oddly, despite Prince Albert's complaint that American women appeared too frequently in the newspapers, Alice Heine was almost totally ignored by the American press. She was so unknown in her own country that of the few newspapers which published a brief paragraph on her death, some even failed to identify her as having been born in the United States.

But if she escaped the notice of the American press, she had not gone unnoticed by wealthy American families with eligible daughters who also were not averse to a French title. Within a few years after Alice had become the Duchess of Richelieu, and continuing to 1914, so many other American girls married Frenchmen of the high nobility that historian Henri Bellamy wrote:

"One is struck by the fact that all these young misses from overseas, with very rare exceptions, picked their husbands among what we call *'la bonne noblesse,'* and even the very good ones. One has the impression that the young ladies carefully checked their suitors' credentials before they went to the altar, and made sure not to buy 'the cat in the bag.' "

Needless to say, they followed the firm French custom that the bride brings along with her a handsome dowry. The record was believed to be set by Miss Adela Sampson, who married Duke Charles Maurice de Talleyrand-Perigord and whose dowry was reported to have been seven million dollars, though Miss Helen Morton, who married the Duke de Valençay et Sagan, was a runner-up with six million dollars. Many of these American brides became friends with Alice.

Two daughters of Isaac Singer, who piled up millions with his sewing machines, married into the French nobility. Winnaretta, a moody, melancholy woman, first was married to a baron, and then in 1893 became the Princess de Polignac. She loved music, was very generous to young musicians and since she and Alice shared similar musical tastes, they became very close friends. Her sister, Isabel, married the Duke de Decazes, supplying a well-publicized dowry of two million dollars. He was considered somewhat of a snob. One day while he was at the Monte Carlo Casino, he showed his displeasure when he was seated next to Alexandre Duval, who was not of nobility but who had piled up millions as the owner of a popular French restaurant chain.

Duval caught the look of disdain on the duke's face, and to the amusement of the others at the table he remarked, "Why, we can very well gamble together, my dear Duke. After all, we both have the same ancestry. We are both Ducs de la Restauration."

Another American woman who married a Polignac was Nina Crosby, who previously had been married to James Biddle Eustis, American Ambassador to France from 1893 to 1897. She became Marquise de Polignac. The marquise is the grandmother of Charles Eustis Bohlen, present United States Ambassador to France. Prince Rainier of Monaco is related to the Polignac family; his father is Prince Pierre de Polignac.

Mattie Mitchell, who married the Duke de La Rochefoucauld, the same family into which Alice's daughter Odile married, was considered the most beautiful of all American women in France. Her dowry was comparatively small, only $300,000. She had rust-colored hair and light green eyes. After the death of her husband François, she always dressed in mauve. Andrew de Fouquières called her a "fairy-tale creature" and said, "Her charming face had all the graces of a Nattier model." Nattier was a noted French portrait painter of the eighteenth century.

Many other American women married into the French nobility while the former Alice Heine was the leading hostess. Some of them, with the reported amounts of their dowries, are Miss Diana Forbes, $1,000,000, wed to the Duke de Choiseul; Miss Clara Coudert, $250,000, the Marquis de Choiseul; Miss Beth Spirry, $500,000, Prince André Poinatowski; Miss Isabella Andrews, $800,000, Count de Pourtales; Miss Carola Livingstone, $800,000, Count de Laugier-Villars; Miss Amie Cutting, $550,000, Baron de la Vrillère; Miss Helen Thomas, $200,000, Viscount d'Aigremont; Miss Blanche Fischer, $250,000, Count d'Aramon; Miss Ella Thorndike, $200,000, Count de Sartiges; Miss Litta Garner, $4,000,000, Marquis de Breteuil. The marquis's son continued the tradition of marrying an American woman when he succeeded to the title, and his bride was the former Miss Julia Woodley.

Today the children and grandchildren of these alliances of ancient French titles and American women make up a large part of the guest list at each gala in the Monte Carlo Sporting Club.

CHAPTER 4

Russian Caviar

If Russian Communists today are conspicuous by their absence from Monte Carlo, it may be that they are following the word of their patron saint, Karl Marx. The German-born author, then living in London, vacationed at the fun center in 1882 and, needless to say, disapproved of what he saw. Incidentally, this was his last vacation; he died the following year.

In a letter from Monte Carlo to his daughter Tussy, the founder of communism compared the Principality of Monaco to Jacques Offenbach's operetta state of Gérolstein when he wrote: *"The economic basis of Monaco-Gérolstein is the gambling house; if it were closed tomorrow, Monaco-Gérolstein would sink into the grave—all of it."* At that time Offenbach's *La Grande-duchesse de Gérolstein* was a very popular light opera.

But if Marx and his disciples did not like Monte Carlo, the assorted grand dukes and others from Czarist Russia most certainly did. They were perhaps the gayest and zaniest of all nationals who went there regularly, and for sheer opulence of living set a mark that has never been equaled at the resort.

The Russians were aware of Monaco even before the casino opened, but their interest then was more pragmatic. Russia at that time was one of the great sea powers, and the czar felt that the Rock would make a sort of Gibraltar for his fleet. It was no secret that the ruling Grimaldis were perpetually in financial difficulties, and the czar felt that the sight of some solid gold rubles would overwhelm them, and they would sell the principality to him. And as a gentle coercive force, he decided to send a squadron of his fleet there under the command of Admiral Popoff, who would conduct the negotiations. Grand Duke Nicolas, the czar's brother, was to vacation in nearby Nice so that he could be at hand if needed as an adviser.

Admiral Popoff and his flotilla sailed in November, 1858, and on the morning of December 6, the warships, emblazoned with the cross of St. Andrew, appeared on the horizon. Long before the vessels finally anchored in the harbor, it was obvious even to a landlubber that the seamanship being displayed by the approaching vessels was erratic. Some zigged while others zagged; they crossed and recrossed each other's bows, narrowly avoiding mishaps.

Grand Duke Nicolas was one of the observers on shore. He hurriedly obtained a boat and headed for the flagship. Although the sea was calm, almost everybody on board, including Admiral Popoff, was staggering about as if the vessel were caught in a raging storm. The same was true on ship after ship. Virtually the entire crew was gloriously drunk. The naval vessels had stopped en route at Piraeus, the port of Athens, and exchanged barrels of cannon grease for barrels of wine, which they had sampled. The smooth-tasting nectar seemed mild to them, a mistake many people have made.

The entire personnel, including the admiral, were ordered

confined to ship for forty-eight hours, with punishment of death for any disobedience. When Nicolas returned two days later, he was greeted with a 24-gun salute and by a trim, smart but badly frightened crew. A contrite Admiral Popoff had prayed an entire night in front of an icon and had punished himself by directing his chief mate to give him twenty lashes with a whip across the back.

Satisfied with his inspection, the grand duke ordered Admiral Popoff to carry on with his negotiations. But the Grimaldis, who had hung grimly to their barren acreage century after century, would not even discuss the possibility of selling themselves out of the royalty business. Admiral Popoff then offered to have Russia finance the construction of a railroad line to Nice in exchange for a long-term lease of the harbor, but this offer also was rejected, and the admiral sailed back with his flotilla.

Though Admiral Popoff may have accidentally started the tradition of Russian carousing at Monte Carlo, it was Grand Duke Michael Nikolaiev, a brother of Czar Alexander II, who made it the fashionable resort for his countrymen when he discovered the joys of wintering there instead of facing the rigors of his native land. The grand duke was one of Russia's wealthiest men; his holdings included the mineral springs of Tiflis, whose bottled water was sold all over the world. He always traveled in a private train that contained six salon cars, but because he had a heart condition, engineers were not allowed to go faster than thirty miles an hour. Twice a year, at the start and close of the Monte Carlo season, railroad traffic would be hopelessly snarled in vast sections of the continent. His poky nonstop train always was given the right-of-way—not even a crack express was permitted to pass ahead of the grand duke's private train.

Because of his poor health the grand duke lived a somewhat sedate life in Monte Carlo, but his son Michael more than made up for it. Together with his cousins Paul, Serge and George, the younger Michael set the Russian tone on the Riviera for several decades. He always was madly, passionately in love with some woman, showering her with expensive jewels, and there usually was a long line of women waiting hopefully on the sidelines, wanting to be next. He was a tall, elegantly dressed man, with a small goatee. As the years advanced, he dyed this blond in order to look younger.

The public was not told that he was living in exile. He had courted Countess Ignatiev, a member of Russia's lower nobility. The czar would not approve the match, and Michael was sent abroad for an extended visit to cool off. He was in Cannes the following year, still on tour, when he met a young German girl named Sophie von Merenberg, and they were secretly married in San Remo. When the czar finally learned about it, he ordered his nephew's name stricken from the royal grants and forbade him to return to Russia.

The edict was of no particular hardship to the grand duke. His father had died; he had succeeded to the title and had inherited 30 million rubles, enough money to continue his merry way. He built a sumptuous villa which he named Kazbek, after the highest mountain in the Caucasus. The mansion was so large that it since has been divided into ten huge luxury apartments. His home quickly became the meeting place for kindred souls, and it was here that King Edward VII was introduced to Mrs. Alice Keppel, who later became His Majesty's companion.

The Russians were serious drinkers. Many started the day with eight glasses of porto, a sweet wine, simply to get into a good mood. It was a rare evening when at least one of them did not toss empty bottles at the huge and expensive mirror behind Betteloni's Bar. This mirror had to be replaced daily; it was a point of honor that the damage had to be paid promptly. Prince Galitzine was so fearful that he might become parched on his way from his hotel to the casino that he always kept several flasks of champagne in his carriage. His hotel was a leisurely five-minute drive from the gaming tables.

The Russian nobility lived on a lavish scale, spent prodigious sums of money, and their losses at the casino ran into the millions of francs in one night. Those who stopped at hotels were not content with mere suites; they rented several floors at a time in the most luxurious hotels. Many of them had villas containing from fifty to sixty rooms, but even far into this century few of these homes were equipped with bathtubs or indoor plumbing. Each season meant a fresh flood of gold coins to natives in the area, since the Russians employed many local servants as well as brought serfs with them.

Grand Duke Michael's permanent staff included two butlers, a housekeeper, two chambermaids, six cooks and eight footmen in livery; these wore white knee stockings and powdered wigs. Additional servants were hired when he entertained.

But even the lavish spenders were miserly compared to the profligate Prince Tscherkassky. He started each season by hiring a minimum of eighty-seven servants, forty-eight of them gardeners. The prince loved growing flowers but could not bear to look at the same variety more than once. Every night, after he went to bed, his gardeners came to work, and they had to change completely all flower arrangements in the large grounds of his villa. This had to be done quietly, without arousing the sleeping prince. His first act upon arising was to rush to the window and study the new floral displays. If the arrangements did not please him, there would be wholesale dismissals. The gardeners who were able to finish out a season usually were able to retire for life. They rented the plants they used from local greenhouses, but the prince paid the full price.

One grand duke succeeded in disrupting a Monte Carlo Opera performance of *Tosca*. He arrived well fortified with his favorite beverage, and also carried an ample supply with him. During intermission he decided to go backstage to offer his congratulations to the diva Wanda Kuznetzoff, as world-famous then as Callas is today. When the nobleman arrived in the dressing room, the singer made the customary curtsy. The duke stared down at her and was diverted from his original thoughts. He blurted, "Madame, you really have a magnificent bosom."

The singer hurriedly straightened up and pretended that she had not heard him, but the duke had a one-track mind. "I must say, though," he added thoughtfully, "it looks suspicious to me."

The curtain never went up for the next act. A physician had to be summoned to quiet the hysterical diva, and the remainder of the performance was canceled.

The distaff side of Russian nobility also cavorted in Monte Carlo. The most notorious of all was Grand Duchess Anastasia Michaelowna, the mother of the last German crown princess.

She had so many affairs with younger men that she was irreverently nicknamed "The Dragnet." Whenever she entered the casino, she always looked around for new young pages, waiters and croupiers. At one time she began to wear shapeless sack dresses, and said she had a stomach tumor. Several months later she gave birth to a son, who later became a wealthy wine merchant in London.

While her own relatives looked on with tolerant amusement, the kaiser was more sensitive, and he would dispatch an emissary now and then to Monaco to tell her to be more discreet, at least in public. He made the error, at first, of sending handsome young men as messengers, but after Anastasia welcomed them with very wide open arms, he switched to elderly courtiers. They were equally unsuccessful, but at least added no new scandals.

With the outbreak of World War I, Grand Duchess Anastasia remained on the Riviera. She wrote to her son-in-law, the German Crown Prince, telling him that it was silly to war against France. He replied by return mail, curtly advising her to stay out of politics and to keep to her gigolos. When she died shortly after the war, she left her villa Fantasia to a young croupier who had been her most frequent companion during her last years.

Following hard on the heels of the Russian aristocracy were the wealthy Russian merchants and industrialists, snobs at heart, who were hoping that their riches would help break down the caste barriers that were so rigid in their native land. They knew it was hopeless within their own country, but in Monte Carlo, with its more relaxed atmosphere, they thought they might have a chance. Even to be seen in casual conversation with a member of the nobility they considered a major triumph. If they had an eligible daughter, they were certain to bring her along. If not, the contacts were good for business. But there were few impecunious Russian noblemen in those days, and the gatecrashers were rarely successful. The antics of many of these millionaires added to the Russian lore of Monte Carlo.

One of the regular visitors was a man named Apraxin, a Caucasian millionaire, who arrived each November 15 and departed regularly every March 15. He always employed a string quartet that had to be ready to play for him at any hour of the day or night when he demanded music. Unfortunately, at times, music had a tendency to drive him to suicide, and to guard against it he always had two footmen stationed directly behind his chair. It was their job, at the proper moment, to prevent him from shooting himself or from jumping out of a window.

When such a crisis occurred and the danger had passed, Apraxin would burst into a flood of uncontrollable tears. The only cure was a potion brewed specially for him in the perfume town of Grasse. This consisted of a mixture of cognac, violet liquor and heavily sugared Heidsieck champagne. After downing from eight to ten goblets of this, the millionaire would pass out and wake up fresh the following morning.

Native Monégasques always looked forward to the visits of Simon Malutine, a wealthy Moscow insurance broker. He liked to stand at the open window of his hotel room and fling out gold coins in order to watch the people below fight for the money. The Sanines, a family of fur traders, were even more extravagant. Each winter they rented an entire floor of the Hôtel Splendide. Their party never included less than forty persons when they registered, since they brought their own serfs with them, but there were always vacant bedrooms because the serfs had to sleep in the corridors in front of their masters' chambers. The Sanines were heavy gamblers and rarely returned from the casino before 3 A.M. The hotel had a standing order to have a cold buffet waiting for them in a salon—champagne, caviar and pâté de foie gras. Quite often they went to bed without touching the food, and the same dishes were served to them again and again, but whether they ate the food or not, they were charged for the repast every night.

One year Princess Suvorov, a descendant of the great field marshal, took pity on these hopefuls. After a winning night at roulette she walked out of the casino with 150,000 francs, and decided to celebrate her coup by bringing together the aristocracy and the commoners. She soon expanded her idea and decided to hold a prince and pauper ball. Not only would she bring together the aristocracy and the millionaires, but she decided to invite all the socialites on the coast, plus a liberal sprinkling of demimondaines and gigolos. She engaged a hotel ballroom, but when the owner learned the kind of party she had planned, he indignantly canceled the contract. Other hotels also refused accommodations, fearing a scandal.

The party seemed doomed, but at almost the last moment the princess learned that Villa Mimosa, a beautiful mansion, had remained vacant for the season because the absentee owner had asked too high a rental. The place also was up for sale.

Princess Suvorov hurried to the real-estate agent and informed him that she wanted to rent the villa for just one night. The bewildered man could not understand it at first, but when he learned the details of the ball, he decided to cut in on her roulette winnings and demanded 5,000 francs, then worth $3,200, for the rental of Villa Mimosa from 7 P.M. to 7 A.M. The princess agreed.

This ball is still talked about in Monte Carlo. The wine was flowing freely, and the ill-assorted guests were having such a good time that Princess Suvorov dreaded having to turn them out at the 7 A.M. deadline. She decided the only way out of her dilemma was to buy the mansion immediately. The real-estate agent, routed out of bed in the middle of the night, arrived in dressing gown and slippers. He quickly drew up a contract selling Villa Mimosa to the princess for 120,000 francs. The documents were signed shortly before seven o'clock, and the triumphant new owner announced to her guests that the party would continue.

One of the guests, pointing to the slipper-clad real-estate broker, suggested a slipper toast. All of those present—members of the nobility, prostitutes, officers, pimps, diplomats

—took off their shoes, filled them with champagne and drank to the health of the new owner.

There was an ironic twist to this episode, one that can give scant comfort to moralists, and one that still pleases Monégasques. When the Russian Revolution occurred, Princess Suvorov, by then an elderly lady, managed to escape and made her way to the Riviera. She had lost all her possessions, but she still owned Villa Mimosa, a souvenir of a ball-night whim. By subletting the beautiful mansion for ten months a year, she was able to live out her life in comfort.

After the war the casino checked on what had happened to its former Russian clients, and learned that 430 out of 650 had died a violent death. A few of the survivors, most of them penniless, came back to Monte Carlo as refugees, and Camille Blanc, owner of the casino, remembering the millions they had gambled away at his tables, named them "technical advisers," and granted them small monthly payments. Simon Malutine, the man who had tossed gold coins out of his hotel window, drew such a pension until he died in 1935.

Although the end of the war brought an end to the madcap Russian aristocracy, it did not end the Russian cultural contributions to Monte Carlo. All through the war, the casino, even though its revenues had been cut sharply, continued to pay all its employees serving with the Allied Armies, expecting that business would pick up once there was peace. The ballet was revived and Sergei Diaghilev, who had spent the war years in Spain and South America, was brought back. He created such new ballets as *Aurora's Wedding* and Stravinsky's *Night People*. He also brought forward a great new male dancing star, Serge Lifar. Serge was eighteen when he fled from Saint Petersburg, sought out Diaghilev and told him he wanted to become a second Nijinsky.

The great Nijinsky was in a mental institution, and his

sister was giving ballet lessons in Monaco. Lifar was sent to her, and within a few months made his first appearance with the Monte Carlo Ballet.

He recently recalled his early days as he rose to stardom:

"I never slept. Instead I went out to the Monte Carlo jetty and danced all night alone between the two light towers. In the morning, I climbed up to La Tourbie to watch the spectacle of the rising sun. Then I ran all the way down to the casino because I was afraid to be late for rehearsals. Diaghilev soon saw that I was wasting my strength and blamed the girls for it, of course. All my denials didn't help and, from then on, he saw to it that I was in bed at 11 P.M. every working day."

But as the casino soon found out, the war also had largely wrecked the European society upon which it had depended. Revenues continued to drop, and Prince Albert of Monaco became restive at his loss in income. The reign of the Blancs as owners of the casino, begun by Camille's father, was to be over. A new era soon was to begin when the playground of kings would give way to being the playground of the people.

For the past few years Monégasques have watched with interest the arrival of small groups of tourists from Communist Russia, particularly during the Cannes Film Festival. Although these visitors have been few in number and have not entered the casino itself, some Monégasques are hopeful that once more the Russians will be coming to Monte Carlo. They point out that even Karl Marx came to look and that his disciples should follow in his footsteps.

CHAPTER 5

Systems and Superstitions

One of the tourist sights in Monte Carlo is the equestrian statue of Louis XIV in the entrance to the Hôtel de Paris. Visitors always smile at the way the horse's knee has been worn almost smooth by the caresses of countless superstitious gamblers on their way to the casino. And more than a few of the laughing sightseers will run their fingers across it in the guise of testing its smoothness, and then quickly enter the casino themselves, while considerate hotel attendants hold their smiles.

Gambling and superstition are more than closely allied; they have been hand-holding partners since man shifted his challenge from wielding a skull-cracking weight to placing a bet, and the casino even caters to this. A gypsy fortune-teller is allowed to ply her trade within the building, but she cannot predict winning or lucky numbers, only general information as to whether the inquirer will be lucky or unlucky that night. It is a most happy situation for the soothsayer; all she has to do is be gloomy and seldom be wrong.

The paint was hardly dry on the walls of the newly opened casino when players began to bring their endless variety of charms, talismans, mystic motions, maneuvers and sitting positions, all designed to foil the immutable laws of mathematics.

One of the earliest visitors who caused an uproar was an Italian countess who mixed reverent piety with irreverent greed. In preparation for her visit to the casino she went to the Vatican, where she induced an official she knew to place a gold louis among the rosaries, medals and other items to be blessed by the Pope, pretending she wanted it for a charitable purpose. Convinced that this coin now would ward off the evil of too many losing numbers, she journeyed to Monte Carlo and used it to make her bets, always removing it and substituting another coin when the spin of the roulette wheel went against her.

Her lucky coin seemingly worked for two days, and she was ahead. On the third day her attention was distracted at the moment the ball dropped into a slot, and the croupier promptly raked in the bets of the losers, her coin among them. Her shrieks stopped further play as she frantically searched through the pile, but she had neglected to place any identifying mark on her particular lucky piece, and one gold louis looked very much like another.

The determined countess returned home prepared to get another coin blessed, but news of her impious act already had reached Rome, and she received such a tongue-lashing from the high-placed churchman she had duped that she is said to have entered a convent. At least, she did not return to the casino.

Author Adolphe Smith encountered an unusual form of good-luck charm, unusual even for Monte Carlo. He was seated next to a vivacious widow who was having a winning streak, and he congratulated her on her lucky run. The woman opened her purse and told him to look inside for the answer. The handbag contained some silver coins, similar to those the woman was using in placing her bets, and on the bottom he noticed a slimy gray mass, about the size of a 10-cent piece. Unable to identify it, he asked her what it was.

"It's the heart of a bat," was her unexpected reply. She explained that she had paid a porter to catch and kill one of the bats that roosted in the railroad freight yards, then had taken it to her hotel room and removed the heart herself. She gaily informed Smith that she had had to pay the porter only ten francs for the flying mammal because he had not known its true value; she would have been willing to pay much more. All the coins in her purse that rubbed against the bat's heart were lucky ones.

Keeping a straight face, Smith asked the widow if she would allow him to drop one of his gold coins on the bat's heart to see if some of its magic might rub off for him. He never knew whether his voice betrayed him, or if he really had selected the wrong coin. The woman glanced at him sharply and then said, "It is my mistake, of course. I had the impression that you were a brother, a fellow initiate. The bat is a creature of the moon, she corresponds to the feminine in nature. Her metal is silver, so how can you expect a bat to influence gold, the metal of the sun?"

Gamblers look for signs everywhere, as the Reverend Taylor, pastor of the Anglican church in Monte Carlo, found out. There was a sudden upsurge in Sunday attendance, so much so that he began to think of the need for constructing a larger building. But the pastor also knew his Monte Carlo. He telephoned the director of the casino and asked him if he had heard anything that could account for the increased popularity of his sermons. Camille Blanc was equally puzzled, but said he would have his men investigate. The answer was soon supplied. Several weeks earlier the minister had selected Hymn No. 36 for his congregation to sing. A visitor from South Africa, present at the services, looked upon the number as a signal from heaven. Immediately after he left church he went to the casino, staked 2,000 francs on 36 and won. He could not resist talking about it; and as word spread among the gamblers, they joined the faithful flock each Sunday, waiting for the number of the hymn. Even though the pastor's selections had not been that lucky in the next two weeks, the gamblers still came hopefully. With this information, Rev. Taylor promptly made it a rule that no hymn under No. 37 would be selected, and since the highest number on the roulette wheel is 36, attendance at Sunday services quickly returned to normal.

Many men prefer a more lively talisman, like a pretty blonde, brunette or redhead of the evening. These girls always fervently wish for their escorts to have a winning night the first time they go out with him. They know from experience that if he does win, he will regard them as a good-luck charm and will insist upon their company any time he goes to the casino after that. Not only are they able to raise their fees, but they also can wheedle a handful of chips at a time when these stack high in front of him. One pretty blonde wound up with $25,000 when her companion had a good run of luck for several days. By the end of the week he had lost all his money; the girl wisely had banked her nest egg.

Superstitions are individual whims and seldom affect the amount of money a player will gamble, but it is the system player who brings an anticipatory gleam to the eyes of casino officials. Once a person thinks he has an infallible system, he will bet far more heavily than the others.

In the days when fabulous fortunes were won and lost at its tables, the casino dreaded just one kind of publicity, stories about suicides. Not only did they stir up agitation against gambling, but they had a depressing effect on players, and many stayed away.

A young Italian girl started just such a chain reaction. Eleonora Duse, the great actress, was appearing nightly in the theater and after her performance, would go to the gaming rooms, where she would lose the salary being paid her —in itself, one reason why Monte Carlo did not mind paying stars high salaries, as Las Vegas hotels have since learned. On this night Duse was seated next to a pretty young girl who became increasingly agitated as her pile of chips dwindled. The actress, noticing the girl's distress, told her to take it easy, but the girl brushed her aside, placed something in her mouth and a short time later slumped over in her chair. She had taken a quick-acting poison and was dead.

Deeply shaken by what she had just witnessed, La Duse stood up, announced in her ringing voice that she would never gamble again and walked out of the casino. And she kept her word. Other celebrities soon followed. Isadora Duncan, who always made Monte Carlo one of her stops on her world dancing tours, also vowed to stay away from the gaming tables.

The worst blow for the casino was yet to come. Sarah Bernhardt was then the great public idol. Few people knew that she was a compulsive gambler. She lost huge amounts at the Monte Carlo Casino, but because she earned large sums, no one paid any attention. Actually, her losses were outstripping her tremendous earnings, and she was in debt.

The casino was still unsettled by the bad publicity it had been receiving when the Divine Sarah entered one night. In her purse was the last of her remaining capital, 100,000 francs. She was determined to stake it all that night in an attempt to recoup her losses. Three hours later the entire sum had been lost.

Sarah returned to her room in the Hôtel de Paris and took an overdose of sleeping powder. Fortunately, a short time later, one of her friends, the Vicomte de Rohan, called at her suite, discovered what had happened and quickly summoned medical aid. When she recovered, he lent her 300,000 francs, and Sarah Bernhardt joined the ranks of those who stayed away from the casino. American Princess Alice, wife of Prince Albert of Monaco, was a friend of Sarah Bernhardt's, and her banker father, Michael Heine, took charge of the actress's finances. Within six months she was able to repay the loan, and the financier made shrewd investments of her earnings, so that when she finally retired from the stage, she was a wealthy woman.

The suicide attempt of Sarah Bernhardt was too important a story for Blanc to hush up completely, and as a result some of the heavy losers became more cautious, and casino revenues began to drop.

It was at this low ebb that Charles Wells, a short, paunchy cockney, came to the casino in July, 1891, and won fame as the man who broke the bank of Monte Carlo. He gave the casino a much-needed shot in the arm. He said he was an inventor and had patented a musical rope that had been a fad in London. The total capital he had brought with him was 10,000 francs; many of the titled and wealthy regulars at the casino risked more than that on one spin of the wheel.

Wells started out cautiously, but in the parlance of the gambling fraternity, he was "hot." No matter what he played, black or red, or the full numbers, he was winning with almost monotonous regularity. He increased his betting to 2,000 francs at a time, doubling his stakes each time he lost, until they reached the maximum.

Excitement swelled in the casino when he broke the bank. Actually it was not the casino bank, but the bank at the table where he was playing. Each table started the day with a cash reserve of 100,000 francs. If a player succeeded in winning this money, the wily Blanc had devised a ceremony to call attention to this feat and give a psychological lift to the losing players. A black cloth was draped over the table, and it was momentarily out of play until guards marched up in ostentatious display with a fresh bankroll.

Pandemonium broke out when, for the second time in one day, Wells again broke the bank. Members of nobility clawed at each other as they fought to get close to the table and make the same bets Wells was placing.

The *chef de parti* Bertollini, who supervised the play at Wells's table, said later of this conduct, "The worst thing was the greed that his success aroused in the other guests. They crowded around his table eight ranks deep, and all wanted to play the same numbers he did. They would shout at my croupiers in English, German, French, Italian, Indian and Kurdish. In the end, I could do nothing else but limit the number of players at the table. That led to new violent clashes with persons who thought I was afraid they might win too much."

Wells seemed to be operating with a purposeful system. All the full numbers he bet on were under 10, and he made most of his bets on 1 and 2. He would let his winnings stand for three consecutive runs. Notetakers were standing on chairs, scribbling on charts like mad, and these were being sold to those on the fringes who could not get close to follow the play.

His stamina equaled his luck. He remained at the table for eleven straight hours until he finally called it a day. Croupiers stared with disbelief the next morning when Wells turned up at the opening hour. Although the casino opened at ten o'clock, this usually was for the small bettors; the wealthy did not consider it fashionable to appear until after dinner and the theater. By 3 P.M., the unfashionable Englishman in a hurry had broken the bank for the third time. By now the Russian grand dukes and a king or two had rushed to watch what was going on, and newspaper reporters were sending the story all over the world. The bad publicity the casino had been receiving faded out in the excitement.

The run of luck continued on the third day, and by that night Wells had won one million francs. He stopped playing roulette at that point and made for the door to cash in his chips. As he passed a baccarat table, he couldn't resist making a few more bets. In the next half-hour he accumulated another 150,000 francs.

Wells returned to England, where he was greeted as a national hero. He gave lavish parties, patronized the best supper clubs and tipped heavily.

Although some casino officials were alarmed when they saw Wells depart with all that money, Camille Blanc was not worried. He predicted that Wells would be back. "We'll get our money back," he assured them.

Part of his prediction came true in November when Wells again returned to Monte Carlo, but the Englishman picked up where he had left off. He started out by placing 1,200 francs on number 5, and let it ride for five successive spins. Five came up five times in a row and Wells, in a matter of minutes, had won 98,000 francs.

Even Blanc was staggered at the news. He began to suspect collusion and that night called the croupiers into his office and questioned them thoroughly. He finally assigned ten of his best detectives to watch Wells every moment and to keep a sharp eye on the wheel and the croupiers at the table. They were to report to him twice a day. History repeated itself, and again in three days Wells won another million francs and left the casino. The detectives had absolutely nothing to report; there had been no signals exchanged, no tampering with the wheel. Wells's winnings had been legitimate.

By now, the most phenomenal run of luck in the casino's history was a page-one story wherever newspapers were published. That winter, Charles Coburn introduced the song

"The Man Who Broke the Bank at Monte Carlo," in a London revue, and the song became a hit in England, spread throughout the Continent and soon was being sung, hummed and whistled in the United States.

People everywhere talked of the nobody who had won a fortune at Monte Carlo, and debated his system. They could make little sense of the published charts of some of his plays; only he had the key, and he refused to discuss it. The loss that the casino had suffered was really a windfall since it made Monte Carlo a household name.

Once again Wells went on a wild spree when he returned to London. He was picked up by society, wore tails and a top hat; and wherever he made his entrance, the band was certain to play "The Man Who Broke the Bank at Monte Carlo."

Wells made his third appearance at the casino during the 1892 winter season, arriving in a style suitable for a man of his importance, aboard the yacht *Palais Royal* and accompanied by his mistress Joan Burns, an artist's model from Chelsea. When he seated himself at his favorite roulette table, Camille Blanc served personally as *chef de parti,* the man who supervises the play at the table. The bubble burst for the little Englishman—and he lost steadily. He cabled to London for fresh funds, which he also lost.

But Charlie Wells was not gambling his own money. He had squandered his winnings in riotous living. The little cockney was a small-time crook and confidence man, and had talked his newly found rich friends into backing an invention he claimed to be perfecting, a fuel-saving device for steamships. Among his dupes were the son of Lord Ashton and a sister of Lord Phillimore. The yacht he was using had been chartered by his backers, supposedly for test trials of his nonexistent device. When he lost at Monte Carlo, he had taken the precaution of wiring his backers for more money from neighboring Ventimiglia, rather than Monaco, stating that his machine was out of order, and he needed the money rushed for repairs. It was after Wells sailed from Monte Carlo that his victims learned that he had been gambling. He was arrested aboard the yacht at Le Havre and extradited to England. After being convicted on a charge of obtaining some $150,000 under false pretenses, the man who broke the bank of Monte Carlo was sentenced to eight years in prison.

One person remained faithful to him, his mistress Joan Burns. When he had served his sentence, she met him at the prison gates, and they went to Paris. Here he developed a scheme Ponzi later was to use with great success in the United States. He advertised that he would pay one per cent interest per day on funds left with him. The few lucky persons who were among the first investors were promptly paid their daily interest; this started the bandwagon rush, and some 60,000 Frenchmen had been fleeced when Wells was finally arrested, once again aboard a yacht. He later died in poverty in Paris.

If it was Edward VII, while he was the Prince of Wales, who made Monte Carlo fashionable with royalty and the millionaires, it was the little trickster, with his fabulous run of luck, who made the casino popular with the well-to-do middle classes. Visitors began swarming in from everywhere, all hoping to duplicate the feat of the man who broke the bank, many of them looking for systems.

Years later Wells admitted that he had had no system, that it had been blind luck; but by then hundreds of books had been published, all containing sure-fire systems and with such intriguing titles as *Life Made Pleasant by Roulette* and *One Hundred Infallible Systems to Win at Monte Carlo.* Noblemen and millionaires were being jostled by shabby figures who became know as "the writers" or "the thinkers." They hovered about the tables, busy jotting down all the winning numbers and deducing from these new infallible methods of winning.

The circulation of a morning newspaper published in Nice began to boom when it started listing the numbers that had come up the previous day in the Monte Carlo Casino. And when the numbers failed to arrive in time, the editors did not want to disappoint their faithful readers, and so they made up lists of winning numbers for the system-players to peruse.

Business boomed at the casino; but, in fairness to Camille Blanc, it must be said that he publicly scoffed at players who believed in systems, and even offered a prize of two million francs to anybody who could present an infallible one. The prize was never claimed.

Theoretically, there is one system with which a player can always come out even in the long run, provided that he has enough money. This is the mother of all systems, the martingale. It requires that each time a player loses, he continue to double his bet until he wins. Since there are men wealthy enough to do that, the casino, from the very first, installed a maximum betting limit, which would prevent anybody from doubling a small stake more than twelve times. With this edge, and a zero which sweeps the board, it is impossible for any system to be infallible. As mentioned earlier, J. P. Morgan once stalked angrily out of the casino because he wanted the limits raised. The casino would have been most happy to make an exception and win his money, but they knew that once they did so, they could be opening the door to future difficulties.

Excitement was so intense after Wells's exploits that Sir Hiram Maxim, the American-born inventor of the one-man machine gun, made a special trip to Monte Carlo to study the possibilities of a system. At his first session at the roulette table, black came out twenty times in a row. Two men next to him were so certain that it was impossible for black to win again that they started betting heavily on red. The wheel spun six more times to black, and the system-players next to Maxim lost 72,000 francs.

He also watched a Dutch planter named Kilian, who did not play himself but hired men to gamble for him. He gave each of them 2,000 francs with instructions that they were not to worry if they lost the money. The puzzled inventor asked the reason for it. Kilian replied, "In order to win, you must dare. Someone who plays with other people's money is much less afraid to run the kind of risks that have to be run if one wants to land a major coup."

Though many of his hired gamblers did lose their stakes, now and then one of them would hit a lucky streak; and Maxim observed such a man turn over 45,000 francs to Kilian. The planter, though, refused to tell whether he was ahead or behind in his strange system.

Maxim finally wrote his conclusions in a letter to the Paris edition of the New York *Herald* in which he said:

"All roulette systems are worthless. If red comes out 20 times, there is no reason why the ball should not fall on red 40 or 70 times. The laws of probability are not valid for this game. Each round offers a 50/50 chance—neither more nor less.

"The ball follows its own law, and this is different every time. Where the ball falls, depends on how it has been thrown, how often it turns around the wheel and which metal pieces it hits on its way. All this is pure hazard and cannot be influenced by anything that happened before or may happen afterward."

The inventor was jeered and denounced by system-players, and the gamblers merrily went on inventing new systems, even though Blanc said bluntly, "The only way of earning money with systems is to sell them to fools."

One of his favorite stories concerned a syndicate of four Parisians who came to Monte Carlo with a substantial fund of 500,000 francs and an ardent belief in their sure-fire system. They were so certain of success that they hired a bookkeeper to keep their accounts.

The malicious goddess of fate was kind to them for three weeks, and their bankroll grew to 1,200,000 francs. They did not want to keep the money in a bank, and so they bought a safe, moved it into their bookkeeper's room and hired a watchman to sit there on the alert with a cocked pistol. The next morning they returned to the room to see how things were going, and the watchman assured them that everything was fine—no strangers had dared come near the safe. But when they opened it, they found it empty. The bookkeeper, who had access to the safe, had rifled it before the watchman came on the job, and had lost all the money gambling while using their system. Blanc paid their carfare home.

A Scottish engineer, William Jaggers, did develop a system that was a nightmare for casino officials until they discovered his secret. He had made a careful study of the construction of the roulette wheel, probing for weak points. Each wheel rested on a steel cylinder whose upper end was hollow. A small metal pin under the wheel fitted into this socket. Jaggers realized that if this pin got worn, a slight deviation would favor certain numbers.

He stationed men at every table to record the winning numbers. This went on for five weeks, and then he noticed that at one table certain numbers came up more frequently than others. He now was ready to play and within four days amassed more than Wells ever won, 2,400,000 francs. The loss to the casino was even greater, since many other players were following his lead.

The casino now began an investigation of its own, and made a record of the numbers Jaggers was playing. That night, after closing time, an unusual game went on in the salon. Blanc and the other directors played the wheel against the house, using Jaggers' list of numbers. They came out 50,000 francs ahead. Blanc promptly ordered the wheels switched on the different tables, and Jaggers began losing when he returned to his particular table the next day. As his losses climbed, the canny Scotsman realized that the wheels must have been switched. He stopped playing and made a leisurely tour of the casino, stopping at each table. With an engineer's eye for detail, he had noticed that his particular wheel had a tiny, barely noticeable scratch on the brass handle. Within an hour he had located his wheel of fortune and resumed winning. Since there was nothing illegal in what Jaggers was doing, the casino was helpless.

At that time the roulette wheels used at Monte Carlo were manufactured in Strasbourg. A casino official hurried there for advice and was told that if the partitions around the little slots in the wheel were changed daily, these would make up for any slight irregularities in the balance of the wheel. The corrective measure worked; and when Jaggers discovered he no longer could predict the numbers the wheel would favor, he lost interest in gambling and left Monte Carlo with a neat profit of 1,200,000 francs.

One of the most unusual system-players was the Irishborn Count of Hammond, who became interested in astrology when he lived in India. Using the professional name of Cheiro, he became a famous astrologer-chiromancist, and his clients included Edward VII, Gladstone, Lord Kitchener and a young reporter of that time named Winston Churchill.

The invention of the roulette wheel has been attributed to Pascal, but Hammond claimed that it existed long before in the Far East as an instrument of occult calculations to determine the rhythm in which figures appear and reappear. He pointed out that the astrologer's zodiac contains 360 degrees while the roulette wheel has thirty-six cases and a zero. In addition, the cylinder of the roulette has four arms dividing the wheel, and the zodiac is divided into four sectors of the year and four cardinal points.

Like all astrologers, he believed that the stars emit radiations that affect the world, and he felt that certain conjunctions or configurations of planets within certain signs could affect the series of figures coming out on the roulette wheel. Hammond would play only one hour at a time after he had established the planetary aspects for that given hour and deduced which numbers and colors would appear during that sixty minutes. He claimed that the numbers 2, 11, 20 and 29 were under the influence of the moon and were therefore feminine, and that was why they were painted black on the wheel, while numbers 9, 18, 21 and 36 were under the influence of Mars, and therefore masculine and so were painted red.

Listeners struggled hard trying to figure out Hammond's system but were completely baffled by it. Nevertheless, each season he appeared in Monte Carlo, gambled only on certain dates and at certain hours, and usually emerged a winner.

The casino was not alone in profiting from system-players. Sam Lewis, a London moneylender, was a familiar figure for years at Monte Carlo, but he did not come to play. He was there to help finance, at a good rate of interest, the titled Englishmen who had run short of funds while backing their latest scheme for beating the wheel. Sam was a snob at heart and liked nothing better than to be invited to the homes of his august clients. One season he was accosted in the lobby of the Hôtel de Paris by an English lord who had had a phenomenal run of bad luck, and was so deeply in debt to the money broker that Lewis refused to advance any further funds.

When the rebuffed nobleman later complained to a friend,

the latter told him to invite Lewis to his castle, which was always good for a loan.

The bankrupt player shook his head. "Not much point to inviting a man to a home he already owns," he replied.

The system-players are still at Monte Carlo, but the center of their activities is not the inner fashionable *salons privés* but the large outer room, known locally as "The Kitchen," which opens every morning and is patronized mainly by elderly retired men and women, living on pensions or small annuities, who rarely gamble more than a handful of francs a day. Many of them sit with notebooks in their hands, making mysterious jottings now and then, and a run of luck that brings in a few hundred francs is cause for wild elation. The casino provides a focal point and serves as a social center for them, and the working out of a system provides them with a pleasant way to pass their time. The casino does not mind; it finds that the steady accumulation of these small wagers makes pleasant reading in the annual financial statement, and treats them with the same deft service and courtesy that would be extended to a millionaire plunger.

It was an American girl named Susan who came up with the best system ever seen at Monte Carlo, one which croupiers still talk about with admiration.

Susan had fallen in love with a Polish count she had met at a party, and she was determined that he would marry her. The count's great love, though, was the roulette wheel. Although she dogged his heels, she could not woo him away from the green baize of the gaming tables. His luck was bad, and he not only lost the money he had inherited, but also began dipping into funds that had been left to him in trust.

When Susan learned this, she rushed to the casino and stood watching from a distance. As she suspected, he was having no better luck this night. She moved closer, and he was so absorbed in his play that he did not notice her standing behind one of the seated players. He was concentrating on color, and Susan quickly pulled money from her purse and began to bet the opposite. He placed 3,000 francs on red, and she made a similar bet on black. Red lost, black won. On the next round, he distributed 6,000 francs over the first and second columns, and Susan placed 3,000 francs on the third column. He lost and she won 6,000 francs.

Her winnings continued to pile up while his chips dwindled. Susan also made bets of her own and hit a winning streak, meanwhile continuing to bet directly opposite the count. The count finally left the table stony broke and started pacing the terrace. When Susan came up to him, he confessed that he had taken the funds from the trust fund and advised her to forget him, since he faced jail.

Susan then told him how she had bet opposite him, thrust the bankroll into his hand and told him, "It's yours. I was winning it back for you."

Although croupiers say that her system is dangerous because a loser can suddenly start winning, they know of no finer system for getting a husband. Susan and the count were married.

CHAPTER 6

Mata Hari's Gamble

One of the greatest gamblers in Monte Carlo's history was a woman, yet she rarely, if ever, made a wager at any of the gaming tables. She gambled her life and lost. Few people know that the casino was the setting where Mata Hari was finally unmasked as a German spy.

With the outbreak of World War I, Prince Albert hopefully declared that his principality was neutral, and to his delight, France accepted the situation. As an enclave within France, with a harbor on the Mediterranean, and near the Italian border, Monte Carlo was ideally situated to become an international spy nest, and it did. Secret agents and devious operators flocked in from Berlin, Moscow, London, Paris and elsewhere.

One of the earliest of these new visitors was Bolo Pasha, a Frenchman, who had received his title from the former khedive of Egypt. Bolo rented an entire floor in the Hôtel de Paris, where he installed a harem of pretty girls and posed as a wealthy, carefree playboy. French counter espionage agents soon established that he was a traitor working for Germany. One of his duties was to try to create a defeatist atmosphere in France. The control of an eight-million-mark deposit the Deutsche Bank had made in the United States was traced to him, and he used some of these funds in an attempt to influence the well-known Paris newspaper *Figaro*.

Paul Bolo also was one of the chief German espionage agents on the Riviera. Pressed by France, Prince Albert allowed Monaco to become a rest center for Allied officers on leave. Bolo's girls were used to pump these officers for information, and the tidbits they gathered helped the spy make shrewd deductions. At first, Bolo used the primitive method of passing this information on by signaling to ships of supposedly friendly neutrals which were cruising offshore. The men receiving this information, then relayed it by wireless to Berlin, using equipment installed on their yachts. The Allies quickly put a stop to that.

Not long afterward, Count Oesterling, an Austrian living in Zurich, in neutral Switzerland, developed an overwhelming passion for flowers from the Riviera. Immense shipments were sent to him several times a week. An ardent theater buff, the count knew many singers and actresses who often went on tour in Germany. He gallantly presented them with bouquets of these flowers each time they took a train going to or through Germany. Artfully concealed in some of the stems were military secrets that had been gathered by Bolo and his operators.

When the flower shipments were stopped, Geneva police became aware that a wealthy Hungarian, Baron Baky, was receiving from Monte Carlo far more oranges than he could possibly use, at least a crate a week. Investigation disclosed that the baron had little interest in the fruit; he usually burned the shipment after carefully removing the thin tissue wrapping around each orange. These tissues were examined and found to contain code messages written in milk. The wrappers were confiscated from each shipment before delivery, but Baron Baky's orders for oranges did not cease; the hidden messages now were being scribbled in a colorless chemical solution on the wooden crates.

But such methods were crude and bungling compared to the techniques of Mata Hari. She did not try to hide her entrance into the neutral principality; in fact, placards telling of her arrival had been posted all over Monte Carlo days in advance. The posters announced that the famous Oriental dancer would appear for a limited engagement in the theater housed in the casino building.

According to legend, Mata Hari was an overwhelmingly beautiful and seductive Eurasian, her origins supposedly shrouded in Oriental mystery. In reality, the actual facts casino authorities compiled about her in their dossier are interesting enough, with no need for myth.

Photographs show that her features were too plain for her to be called even pretty, but she did have lovely arms and legs which she displayed almost completely, since she danced dressed in little more than the forerunner of the G-string, a novelty at that time. Despite her near-nudity, she always kept her breasts covered, but this was not due to modesty. A Paris artist, for whom she had previously worked as a model, said she had had difficulty then getting jobs posing in the nude because she was depressingly flat-chested. In an era when women shunned the sun, she kept her body at an even tan, which helped foster the illusion that she was an Oriental.

Gertrud Margarete Zelle was born in Leeuwarden, Holland. Her father, Adam, a hatmaker, was from Eastern Europe, not East Asia, and her mother was a van der Meulen, a solid bourgeois Dutch family; Mata Hari possessed no Oriental blood whatsoever.

Not long after she graduated from a convent, at the age of sixteen, she met and married a Scottish mercenary serving as a captain in the Dutch Colonial Army. When his leave was up, the newlyweds went to his post at Bengo-Biroe on the island of Java, and it was here that the young bride became interested in the holy temple dances of the Shiva cult.

She watched the natives perform in front of Shiva's gold statue and learned to distinguish among such poetically named numbers as the Dance of the Black Pearl, the Dance of the Holy Flower and the Dance of the Flowing Water. She later was to end many of these ceremonial dances with erotic flourishes whose meaning was clear to onlookers.

Her marriage was not successful. Her husband frequently spent his evenings out drinking with friends and would beat his wife when he came home. One night, after she had gone to bed, he staggered home with three drunken prostitutes, and while his companions watched, pulled Margarete from bed and flogged her with a riding whip. This episode was too much for his superiors, and he resigned his commission. Margarete obtained a separation and went to Paris.

Still young and comparatively fresh, she became an inmate of a luxury brothel near the Gare St-Lazare, but left to become the mistress of a businessman, who established her in a flat in Neuilly. When he went bankrupt, she began working as a model for painters in Montparnasse.

One night, while at a studio party, she entertained her friends by performing some of the dances she had seen in the Java temples. An authority on Eastern culture was present, and he was so impressed by her dancing ability that he promised to arrange a soirée for her. A short time later many prominent Parisians in the world of arts and letters received invitations to attend a gala in the Musée Guimet, Place d'Iéna, on October 12, 1905. The time was set for 10 P.M. Printed in red on a black background, the invitation announced that an Indian bayadere named Mata Hari would perform various temple dances. The Orientalist seems to have been playing his own private joke. He gave Margarete the name Mata Hari and described her as an Indian, but the name is Malayan and means the sunrise.

Joke or not, the party launched Mata Hari on her dancing career, and she became the rage of Paris. She danced in the home of Princess Murat, and in the salons of the Duchess of Richelieu and of the Chilean Minister. Prince del Drago gave a costume ball in her honor, and it was here that she appeared for the first time in the scanty costume that was to become her trademark. The public by now was clamoring to get a look at the dancer who was the talk of the social set, and she made appearances at such leading revue theaters as the Folies Bergères, the Scala and the Olympia. Even so, she still plied her trade, now as a high-priced call girl. Her husband was granted a divorce.

From French society she moved into the world of politics. She was seen with Dutch Minister van der Leyden and then in rapid succession became the mistress of French War Minister Messimy and of Foreign Office head Jules Cambon.

It was in 1907, while on a theatrical tour, that she made her fateful step. She appeared in Berlin for the first time and repeated her Paris triumph. The Duke of Brunswick escorted her on a round of local nightclubs, and the crown prince invited her to accompany him on troop maneuvers in Silesia. Berlin Police Chief von Jagow called to see her at her dressing room; and not long afterward they became lovers and he furnished her with an apartment in the Tiergarten quarter, the best section of the city. When she left Berlin, the money-hungry dancer was a member of the German spy system, Code No. H-21.

As the mistress of the French foreign minister, able to move in similar circles in whatever country or city she appeared, there is little doubt that H-21, Mata Hari, was a most valuable spy for the Germans.

Even before war was declared, British intelligence agents

suspected the dancer and repeatedly warned their French colleagues to check on her. Although they repeated their warning after war broke out and Mata Hari had returned to Paris from Holland, still nothing was done. The foreign minister continued to vouch for her.

The Second Bureau finally began to get suspicious in the spring of 1915, when Mata Hari wangled permission to go to a field hospital in Vittel to nurse one of her numerous male friends, wounded in action at Chemin des Dames. Since the hospital was well staffed with nurses, and the dancer previously had displayed no talent or interest in that direction, intelligence agents had cause to wonder—particularly since Vittel was well in the front zone, where a sharp observer could not fail to notice preparations under way for Marshal Joffre's impending offensive.

The dancer was closely watched upon her return to Paris, but beyond writing letters to relatives in Holland, she seemed to carry on her usual routine; lovers came and went. All letters abroad, of course, were subject to censorship delays, but Mata Hari, because of her friendship with the Dutch official, enjoyed the privilege of using the diplomatic pouch of her native country's legation when she wrote to her family in Holland. The Bureau managed to place one of their agents in the legation, and he read the letters Mata Hari was sending. He could not be sure that they contained coded messages.

Mata Hari left Paris for Madrid, where she was booked for a dance recital for several weeks, and from there she was going to Monte Carlo. Her appearance in Madrid was so successful that she was offered a new contract for the next season and signed it. At the age of thirty-nine the dancer still was bewitching her audiences.

Her schedule provided her with several days off between engagements, and she toured the Riviera in her white

Hispano-Suiza. The war had interrupted the entertainment schedule at Monte Carlo, and she was given a rousing welcome when she arrived. Her most ardent pursuer was Colonel Suvarsky, a handsome Czarist officer on furlough, and they quickly became very friendly.

Each evening after her performance, Mata Hari entered the casino to have a drink. One night, as she did so, the usually impeccable Colonel Suvarsky staggered toward her, obviously intoxicated. He was holding a glass in his hand, and as he neared her, he made an exaggeratedly courtly bow. The other guests watched his conduct with amusement. Suddenly the colonel tossed his glass away, caught the dancer about her waist with his right hand and pressed his mouth on her lips. As he did so, he plunged his left hand underneath the top of her dress.

She managed to break loose, pushed the Russian away and glared at him, her face contorted with fury. Before any of the startled onlookers could make a move, she yanked a tiny silver pistol from her handbag and shot the officer in the chest. When he fell to the floor, she kicked him, deliberately emptied her gun into his body, wheeled and walked away, the perfect picture of an outraged woman preserving her honor.

Suvarsky was rushed to the hospital, where an emergency operation was performed and his life saved. Anguished casino officials, anxious to avoid a scandal, were pleasantly surprised when authorities pointed out that there were sufficient eyewitnesses to prove that the officer had provoked the attack and that accordingly the incident would be hushed up. Mata Hari canceled the rest of her performances and was permitted to leave Monaco.

What was actually being hushed up was that Colonel Suvarsky was a member of the Russian secret service, assigned as a liaison officer with the Allied forces in France. He was

not on furlough but on active duty, and his assignment was
to trap the suspected spy. The plot was hatched while
Mata Hari was in Madrid. Information was leaked where it
would reach the Germans that Colonel Suvarsky, on furlough,
had in his possession top-secret papers on Lenin, Trotsky and
other Russian political exiles. Since the Germans were trying
to stir up trouble inside Russia to relieve the pressure on
them by Russian troops, these papers would be valuable to
them. If Mata Hari was a spy, as they suspected, then she
would receive orders in Madrid to try to get the papers from
Suvarsky in Monte Carlo. To make it even easier for her, the
officer had posed as an ardent admirer.

That afternoon he had entertained Mata Hari at his villa.
He had deliberately delayed her departure until eight o'clock,
knowing that she would have to rush directly to the theater
for her nightly performance. Immediately after she left, he
checked his files and found that she had stolen the reports
on the political exiles.

Unfortunately, at this point, the colonel continued his
lone-hand activities instead of alerting the other agents in the
area. Familiar with Mata Hari's habit of having a night-
cap after her performance, he waited for her at the casino
bar and pretended to be drunk. He reasoned that she had not
had time to dispose of the incriminating documents and so
would hide them in her brassière. He had hoped to catch
her with the evidence, but the quick-thinking woman succeeded, instead, in almost killing him. But the trap had been
sprung. French officials now no longer had any doubt that
Mata Hari was a spy for the Germans. They allowed her to
leave Monaco, hoping that she would lead them to other
members of the spy ring. From that moment on she would be
under constant surveillance by agents of the Second Bureau.

A coded message from Lieutenant von Krohn, the German

military attaché in Madrid, was intercepted. In it he requested funds for H-21 and asked for payment in Paris. Soon
after Mata Hari received the money, she was arrested.

During her trial Mata Hari admitted having received the
funds but denied that she had been paid for being a spy. She
claimed that the payment was for her other well-known
nighttime service.

"Thirty thousand marks for one night?" the astonished
presiding official asked.

"That is my usual fee," was her reply.

But not even the normally gallant Frenchmen could accept
that statement as true, and on October 15, 1917, she was executed by a firing squad.

CHAPTER 7

Zaharoff and the Duchess

During the closing days of World War I, Prince Albert faced
a problem long familiar to the ruling Grimaldis, a lack of
money. The war had cut sharply into the profits of the Monte
Carlo Casino and Monaco's income had taken a corresponding nose dive. Prince Albert needed cash, lots of it, to restore a healthy balance to the principality's faltering ex-
chequer.

Separated from his American wife, Princess Alice, he was
to miss sorely her "head power," as he scornfully described
her business sagacity. Unable to obtain an advance from
Camille Blanc, still the director and the largest stockholder
in the casino, he turned to Basil Zaharoff, the armament king,
the mystery man of Europe; and this move almost cost the
Grimaldis their throne.

Blanc had used the excuse of poor business at the casino
in turning down Prince Albert's request for anticipated earnings, conveniently overlooking his own large personal fortune, which had been made possible by the casino concession. This was a tactical error on Blanc's part. Prince Albert
felt that the drop in casino receipts was due in part to the

aging director's lack of interest; Blanc was paying little attention to the business, and his many affairs with young actresses were being conducted with blatant indiscretion. The prince decided he would oust Blanc at the first opportunity.

But his immediate concern was raising money, and with all the important nations at war, pouring their millions into munitions, he could not turn to any government for a loan. The fortune being spent on munitions turned his thoughts to Zaharoff, who was gathering in much of this money as one of the chief owners of the English armament firm of Vickers. Zaharoff had long been a familiar visitor in Monte Carlo; though he seldom gambled in the casino, he spent much of his free time at the resort.

A short time later Count Balny d'Avricourt, Minister of State of Monaco, hurried to Paris to the Hôtel Ritz, where Zaharoff maintained a suite. He arrived so early in the morning that the armament king was still at breakfast. Old-time hotel employees still shudder at the memory of his unvarying breakfast: four raw eggs.

The visitor discussed Prince Albert's need for a loan, as well as his dissatisfaction with the way the casino was being run, a discreet way of pointing out that by taking over the casino Zaharoff could insure the money advanced. Zaharoff was noncommital. He knew that France, scenting victory, already had drawn up secret plans to annex part of the Italian Riviera, and there had been serious cabinet discussions about annexing Monaco as well, making it little more than a French department. Gambling then was still forbidden in France, and this would have ended the casino.

Zaharoff was conducting important business negotiations with the French Government. At the next meeting it is known that he spoke to Premier Georges Clemenceau, told him about Prince Albert's request and asked if it would be possible for France to guarantee the independence of Monaco after the war. What other conversation was held is not known. But not long after this meeting France, still at war, signed a secret treaty with Prince Albert affirming that Monaco would remain sovereign after the war. This agreement was not made public until a year later at the signing of the Versailles Treaty. It gave France a stronger hold over Monaco.

With the secret guarantee between France and Monaco in effect, Zaharoff advanced Prince Albert one million pounds sterling, $5,000,000, with an understanding that he would take over the casino at the time of his choosing. In this Prince Albert made a tactical error. Although he did not know it—his son Louis II had succeeded to the throne when the pressure began to be applied—the first step had been taken in a long-range plot that is reminiscent of many tired old operettas: a scheme to take over the throne. But it did happen in operetta-like Monaco, and the Monte Carlo Casino was used as a pawn. This modern revival also added a new twist: Zaharoff was not interested in the throne for himself, but wanted to set his beloved lady upon it. The woman was a duchess of the Spanish royal family. And in keeping with the fantastic events of this little-known episode, her romance with Zaharoff is one of the strangest love stories to be found outside of fiction.

Zaharoff, one of the most ruthless and wily men of the first quarter of this century, came out of the slums of Tatavla, in the ancient Greek quarter of Constantinople, to amass one of the world's great fortunes. He was decorated by France and knighted by England, and was a close friend of many of the important political leaders; yet, for more than three decades, neither his enormous wealth nor his tremendous influence could bring about the one thing he wanted most in life—one that most ordinary men achieve—to marry the woman he loved.

To understand the man who engineered this plot, and the

passions that gripped him, it is necessary to know something about his background. He rarely gave interviews, and the few times that he did talk to reporters, he gave out conflicting stories; he either enjoyed deliberately creating an aura of mystery about himself, or else was supremely indifferent to what the public said or thought about him. Many wild and fanciful tales have been printed about his origins, but there is sufficient reliable evidence to indicate that he was a Greek, born in a small town in Asia Minor, and that, while he was a young boy, his merchant father moved to the Tavla district in Constantinople. The family name originally was Zacharias, but during one of the many wars Greece and Turkey fought over Anatolia, his ancestors had fled to Odessa where, for protective coloration, they Russianized their name. They kept the new spelling even when they later straggled back to their own soil.

Zaharoff first came to public attention when he was in his early twenties and the London *Times* noted his arrest. An uncle with whom he had been associated in business in Constantinople filed a warrant charging that his nephew had embezzled funds and fled to England. Court records show he was acquitted.

His version of what had occurred is most dramatic. Through the kindly interest of a wealthy merchant, Zaharoff had been educated in an English-run private school in Constantinople. He later showed such good business judgment that his uncle hired him, and within two years the young man had so increased the business that he demanded, and received, a partnership. His uncle, however, stalled off paying him his share of the profits, and so he waited until the other was away on a trip, took precisely his portion of the money, left a detailed accounting and departed the country. Unable to prove to London police his partnership claim, he was placed in jail to await trial, pending the arrival of his uncle. On the day of the trial the weather turned chilly, and Zaharoff sent for a cloak he kept in a trunk. In a pocket he found the missing partnership agreement. He waited until his uncle took the court oath and stepped on the witness stand. When the prosecutor asked about the partnership agreement, Zaharoff, at this point, shattered usual court decorum by shouting to the judge not to allow his uncle to commit perjury, and produced the agreement. As he had undoubtedly expected, his uncle was so shaken by this sudden development that he admitted the document was genuine, and Zaharoff was freed.

It was a hollow victory for the young man. Zaharoff had come to England hoping to establish a business, but the Greek colony there, disliking the fact that he had abandoned his uncle's business while the other was away, would offer him no assistance. He went to Athens, where he was similarly rebuffed, but he did become friendly with Étienne Skuludis, then rising to prominence in politics. Skuludis, who later became Premier of Greece, came from a similar background, having been born in Anatolia and having spent his youth in Constantinople.

During the next few years Zaharoff shuttled between London and Athens seeking an outlet for his talents, but making little headway until Nordenfeldt, an English armament firm founded by a Swedish engineer, needed a salesman for the Balkan countries. Zaharoff was fluent in many languages, and Skuludis recommended him for the job. His starting pay was twenty-five dollars a week, plus commission.

Nordenfeldt had recently completed the first practical submarine, and Zaharoff patriotically offered it to his own government. Even though Greece was impoverished by a series of small wars, she became the first to purchase a submarine. Actually, Nordenfeldt had tried to sell it to the great powers, but they had been chary of the new weapon and wanted somebody else to try it out first.

With a firm order in his pocket and his patriotic duty done, Zaharoff hurried to Turkey, Greece's traditional enemy, and succeeded in selling the Turks two submarines. He was to develop the pitting of nation against nation into a fine sales art.

Hiram Maxim, the earlier-mentioned Yankee inventor of the one-man machine gun, discovered personally how the resourceful Zaharoff operated. Unable to arouse American military interest in his new weapon, Maxim went to England, where he established a factory, and then set out to conquer Europe, acting as his own salesman.

The inventor arranged for a public demonstration in Vienna before Emperor Franz Josef and the Austrian military leaders. Reporters also were invited to attend. Maxim demonstrated the awesome firing power of his new weapon and, as an added fillip to show its accuracy, he etched in bullet holes the emperor's initials on a wooden board. While the demonstration was in progress, a young man stationed himself with the reporters and offered them a knowledgeable running commentary on the machine gun, which he described as a new Nordenfeldt weapon. The newsmen pointed out that it was supposed to be a Maxim gun, but the stranger was so authoritative that they accepted his word. In the stories they sent to their newspapers, still available in libraries, many of them did describe the weapon as a new Nordenfeldt machine gun.

Zaharoff was not as crude, though, in dealing with the Austrian military leaders, who knew that it was a Maxim gun. He buttonholed them shortly after the demonstration and bubbled enthusiastically about the weapon, meanwhile slyly insinuating that Maxim had to demonstrate it himself because it was too complicated and technical for an ordinary soldier to use; only a mechanically minded Yankee could

operate it, he explained, so it was nothing more than an
interesting toy.

When Maxim appeared at the War Office the next day
expecting to receive a good order, he was surprised at the
exceptionally cool reception he did receive, and it was only
after repeated questioning that he learned how he had been
sabotaged by Zaharoff. The American inventor realized then
that he should concentrate on manufacturing and employ a
good salesman, and the man he wanted was Zaharoff.

Zaharoff recognized that the Maxim gun was the weapon
of the future and urged Nordenfeldt to add it to their line.
Not long afterward, the two firms merged into one; and
since both Maxim and Nordenfeldt were anxious to retain
Zaharoff, he no longer was just a salesman but became one
of the important stockholders in the combined firm, his
territory all of the world. He made his headquarters in
Paris.

The reporters who had been fooled by Zaharoff became
interested in him. Although they were unable to pin him
down to an interview, they followed his movements and
noticed that quite often when a government fell or a revolution or a rebellion broke out, Zaharoff had recently visited
that country. Their stories created a sensation. They soon
had to give up the game when they found that their elusive
quarry had outwitted them again by now employing doubles
who appeared simultaneously in different countries, effec-
tively shielding his tracks.

It was in the fall of 1889, when Zaharoff was forty years
old, that he met the great love of his life. He later told the
circumstances of their meeting to the head of the Monte
Carlo protection force, with whom he became friendly.
Zaharoff was in Saint Petersburg when he received an urgent
message from his home office that Spain was planning to place

a large armament order. Salesmen from all the leading muni-
tion makers in Europe already were wining and dining the
important officials. It was a difficult assignment for Zaharoff
since Spain was one of the few countries where he had no
important personal contacts. He returned to Paris, replenished
his wardrobe and left on the Madrid Express.

That night, while strolling in the corridor of the *wagon-lit*,
smoking his pipe and mulling over his problem, he heard
voices raised in one of the compartments. The door suddenly
opened, and an attractive young girl started out, screaming
for help. An older man, obviously drunk, tried to pull her
back. Because he was hurting the girl, Zaharoff intervened.
Almost six feet tall and with a very erect carriage, he towered
over the other; he separated the couple, and told the drunken
man to go to bed. The latter obeyed. Zaharoff took the
trembling girl to his compartment to wait while he arranged
for separate quarters for her.

Jealous business rivals later claimed that Zaharoff, somehow, must have stage-managed the affair, for he certainly
landed on his feet. The girl, only seventeen years old and
returning home from her honeymoon, was the Duchess of
Villafranca, a cousin of King Alfonso XII of Spain. She
had been married, very much against her wishes, to the much
older duke, who on his honeymoon began exhibiting signs
of a diseased mind.

The duchess apologized to Zaharoff for her husband's
behavior and asked her rescuer to call upon her in Madrid,
an invitation which, in view of Zaharoff's problem, he would
hardly resist. He freely admitted later that it was because
the duchess introduced him into the right circles that he left
Spain with the lion's share of all the orders; in fact, it was
the largest single order of his career up to that time, 150
million dollars' worth of armaments.

Zaharoff stretched out the negotiations for two months

because of another problem; he had fallen deeply in love with the unhappy bride with the musical name: Maria del Pilar Antonia Angela Patrocinio Simona de Muguiro y Beruete, Duquesa de Marquena y Villafranca. And the young noblewoman had fallen as deeply in love with the Greek commoner out of Asia Minor and the slums of Tatavla.

It was a hopeless romance. Divorce was out of the question for a close relative of the king in Catholic Spain. In the eternal pattern of lovers everywhere, they could only pledge each other to wait; someday the sickly duke would die, and they would be able to marry.

Zaharoff was somewhat optimistic. He rented a beautiful apartment on the fashionable Rue de la Bienfaisance in Paris before leaving on a business trip that included South America. The familiar pattern of revolutions and uprisings followed his visit there. There was bad news awaiting him on his return; the duke's mind had completely snapped, and he was locked up in a mental institution. Now Zaharoff no longer could visit Spain, ostensibly on business, to see the duchess. With her husband confined, she could not be seen with another man since it would cause talk.

He gave up his apartment lease, and the two lovers turned to Monte Carlo. The busy resort, with its informal atmosphere and visitors streaming in from everywhere, provided an ideal cover. Although their love affair quickly became known along the Riviera, it caused no scandal abroad, particularly since the gossips had much choicer topics of conversation—the antics of many kings and some of their queens.

They had a brief flurry of hope in 1892, when the mad duke became critically ill. Since Zaharoff would need a birth certificate to get married in France, he sent emissaries to the town where he had been born. They returned with a document that read:

"Zacharias Basil Zaharoff was born in Mugla on October

6, 1849. He was baptized on October 8, by the priest Daniel according to the rites of the Greek Orthodox Church."

It was not an official birth certificate but a statement by three elderly men of Mugla who attested that they had been present in church on the day he was baptized. It was this document that gave rise to the many stories disputing his origins. Zaharoff had no use for it; the duke recovered his health, if not his reason.

The years passed for the lovers. The duchess gave birth to two daughters. Although Zaharoff carried their photographs in his wallet, and their husbands later held important positions in his far-flung enterprises, he never publicly stated or acknowledged that they were his daughters, and the duke's name appears on the birth certificates. Zaharoff did not attend their weddings. There were just two men in the duchess's life: her mad husband, locked up in an institution, and Zaharoff.

He finally made use of his birth certificate in 1908, but not for the original reason. He produced it for the record on his appointment to the French Legion of Honor, and he used it again four years later when he applied for French citizenship. Reporters promptly pointed out that at the time of his arrest in London, he had given Tatavla as his birthplace. The French Government sent Detective Joseph Nadel of the Sûreté to Turkey to investigate. He reported back that Zaharoff had been born in Mugla, and the munitions salesman was granted French citizenship.

While he and the duchess were frustrated in their great desire to be married, Zaharoff was reaching ever higher pinnacles in the business world. Nordenfeldt dropped out of the firm, and Maxim merged with Vickers, England's largest armament maker; Zaharoff became an important stockholder in that firm. He added constantly to his holdings and also branched out into strategic metals, banking, steamship lines and oil in his own private empire that stretched around the world.

Because Monte Carlo held so many important memories for him of his cherished moments with the duchess, the resort virtually became his second home; he would rush there whenever he had free time, whether the duchess could join him or not. The best suite in the Hôtel de Paris was always his, and if he arrived unexpectedly and the suite was occupied, the hotel promptly moved the occupants, whether they liked it or not. He did not even dine on the same plates or use the same service as the other guests; the hotel kept a special set of Limoges dinnerware and a gold service for his exclusive use.

Every wish of his was transformed into a royal command. One day he telephoned Negresco, the owner of the finest hotel in Nice, and complained that no one else knew how to prepare his favorite dish, poule en demi deuil, chicken in half-mourning. He told the hotel owner that he wanted him to come to Monte Carlo every day to prepare the dish for his lunch during the remainder of his three-week stay. Negresco explained that he had stopped cooking long ago, that he was busy running his hotel but would be happy to send an employee. Zaharoff cut him short, told him price was no object—Negresco had to come.

For the next few weeks other guests at the hotel could not decide who looked more crestfallen: Negresco personally serving Zaharoff from a large copper pan he brought with him every day, or the directors of the Hôtel de Paris, who had to watch their most important rival serving their best customer under their roof.

This was the man with whom Prince Albert made the secret compact. Even after he advanced the money, Zaharoff made no overt or public move toward the casino. He was waiting. Meanwhile his agents were secretly buying every share of casino stock offered for sale, all in the name of dummy holders. He still made no move when the war ended.

News of his large loan to Monaco became known, and Camille Blanc, fearing that there might be some move to oust him, returned energetically to the task of restoring the golden flow at the casino. The opera and ballet were revived, and in an attempt to attract new visitors, he instituted the Monte Carlo tennis tournaments for women that were to attract such noted players as Suzanne Lenglen and Helen Wills. He continued the great classic of automobile racing, the Monte Carlo rally.

Zaharoff continued to visit Monte Carlo and seemingly had no interest in picking up his option to take over the casino, nor did he reveal that by now he actually owned the majority shares of stock in the Sea Bathing Society, the controlling corporation. He seemed to be busy with his own affairs. Against the wishes of France, he personally financed an ill-advised and ill-fated war by Greece against Turkey because he wanted to see Anatolia once again a part of Greece; the French backed Kemal Pasha, who emerged the victor. Then he armed the Druses in an oil war around Mossul, and this also was against French wishes. Zaharoff, the citizen of France, became unpopular in his adopted country. In the Senate, Henri de Jouvenel got up and asked, "Who is this international financier who abuses our hospitality? Is he in the pay of the British Intelligence Service? He should be invited to pack his luggage once and for all."

And once again newspapers questioned Zaharoff's origins and his birth certificate. Claims were made that Detective Nadel had been bribed by Zaharoff to bring back his favorable report from Mugla. Nadel had retired from the Sûreté and had been employed at the casino to help spot undesirables and keep them away. Excitement boiled when, in the midst of this, Nadel was found dead in his flat opposite the casino with a bullet in his heart. His death was pronounced a suicide because he had lost 25,000 francs gambling. Some of the sensational newspapers hinted that Zaharoff had had him murdered to prevent him from talking.

If Zaharoff was disturbed by all this, he showed few signs. He did leave on a brief trip to the Balkans, but soon returned to France, alternating his time between Paris and Monte Carlo. Finally, in the spring of 1923, he received the word for which he had been waiting so long—the duke was dying.

Now Zaharoff began to move swiftly. The Monte Carlo Casino was an important part of his plan. By controlling the casino, he was, in effect, controlling the purse strings of Monaco. He could use the casino to try to oust the Grimaldis. But now he needed France on his side; if he took over the casino, France could thwart his plans by denouncing its treaty with Monaco and annexing the principality. On May 14, 1923, he attended a banquet of the Anglo-Persian Oil Company at Claridge's in London. Important leaders were present from France. When the dinner was over, Zaharoff had patched up his difficulties with his adopted country. He had secured for France an important share of the Mossul oil resources. The campaign in France against Zaharoff died down immediately.

Two days later Zaharoff arrived in Monte Carlo and announced that he wanted to take up his option on the casino. The board of the Sea Bathing Society promptly called for a special session for May 18. Camille Blanc was too ill to attend. Zaharoff also stayed away, but his representative produced proxies for 23,000 shares, and Blanc was voted out of office. Alfred Delpierre, an associate of Zaharoff, was named president in his place, and another Zaharoff man, René Léon, was appointed managing director. The Blanc family, which still owned a large block of stock, was allowed to retain one director on the board, Prince Leon Radziwill, a grandson of the founder.

The duke was still alive, and Zaharoff marked time by putting the casino back on a profitable basis. The free show was over at the casino: visitors and players now had to pay an admission fee for the first time in its history. "If people absolutely want to lose money, they'll have to pay for it," Zaharoff said. He understood human nature well, and knew that you could not keep the gamblers away, so they would pay the fee, and sightseers who came to gape at the great and near-great would have no objections to paying for the privilege. He also doubled the minimum stakes. The Blanc family, as a kind of conscience fund, had granted small pensions to unlucky gamblers who had lost their fortunes at the casino, and there were several hundred of them on the payroll. Zaharoff gave them cash settlements, barred them from the casino and removed them from the payroll. Within a few months the casino was prospering again.

On November 23, a cable from Spain announced the death of the Duke of Villafranca. The lovers, at long last, were finally free to marry, but they observed the proprieties; a Spanish duchess could not rush into marriage immediately after the death of her husband. They waited for ten months; and then on September 22, 1924, a long thirty-five years after they had fallen in love with each other and pledged that someday they would marry, they appeared in the small French village of Arronville, near Paris. Zaharoff was seventy-five years old, his once blond hair had turned silvery-white, and because of arthritis, he used a cane. He was dressed all in gray, including a Texas-style hat. The duchess, now a middle-aged woman, her hair streaked with gray, wore a simple dress. As they came to the steps of the town hall, she

gently took Zaharoff's arm and helped him climb the stairs
to the mayor's office. In ten minutes the civil ceremony was
over and the duchess was Mrs. Basil Zaharoff. The cars
returned to the beautiful Château Balincourt, owned by the
duchess, and a religious wedding was performed in its private
chapel. The small wedding party included a son-in-law of
the bride. The newlyweds left on a three months' honeymoon.

When Zaharoff took over the Monte Carlo Casino, newspapers had been astonished; even at its best it was a small
business compared to his vast enterprises. It was estimated
that he had spent 50 million dollars in financing Greece's war
against Turkey without showing the slightest financial
strain. No outsider knew the extent of his fortune. Reporters
speculated that he had made the purchase for sentimental
reasons, delicately hinting at his long-time romance with the
duchess.

But, aside from the duchess, there was little sentiment in
Zaharoff. He had purchased the casino because he wanted to
give her a throne of her own, and upon his return from his
honeymoon he lost little time in putting his plan into
operation. Emissaries made discreet inquiries about the
possibility of the Grimaldis' selling out. They were rebuffed.
Prince Albert had died in 1922, and his son Prince Louis II
was on the throne.

Not long after this a new newspaper, with the ironic name
of *L'Impartial,* made its appearance in Nice. The publisher
was Gaston Grevy, a business friend of Zaharoff's. The paper
quickly started attacking Prince Louis of Monaco, accused
him of having committed fiscal frauds against France and
raked over his private and public life. In thinly veiled form,
the paper was asking that the prince abdicate his throne.

A newspaper battle of words then began. A new weekly

paper, *Tout Va,* made its appearance in Monaco, under the editorship of Sylvain Fabi, and left little doubt as to who was behind the attacks on Prince Louis.

In issue after issue, this paper slashed at Zaharoff. In one editorial Fabi wrote, "There is only one chief in the Principality and that is His Most Serene Highness, Prince Louis II. The others, whether they call themselves Zaharoff, René Léon or Louis Barthou are, after all, nothing but casino types." Barthou was a French politician Zaharoff had placed on the casino board, and Léon, as has been noted, was his personally installed manager of the casino.

Fabi was only warming up to his task. In another editorial he stated bluntly that *L'Impartial* was financed by Zaharoff, whom he described as the *"métèque"* (undesirable alien) of international finance, and added, "Only such rascals can dare attack the ruling Prince, spit on his honor and try to dispossess him. Their maneuver is condemned to failure, but what does it hide? M. Zaharoff is attempting to fish in troubled waters. He has the ambition of playing in Monaco the role of a potentate. Yet Prince Louis has been acknowledged as a sovereign by the League of Nations, and he thus represents a power no one will be allowed to challenge without punishment."

The attack became even more shrill as Zaharoff continued to apply pressure to force Prince Louis off the throne. In an editorial on December 20, 1925, Fabi wrote, "The acts of this powerful financier risk the creation of an atmosphere of turmoil in the principality. Zaharoff one day grabbed the majority of the shares [of the casino] and now thinks he owns the country. He is a revolting autocrat with insatiable appetites, and the valets around him are mere slaves adoring the golden calf."

The continued calls for the prince's resignation suddenly ceased in *L'Impartial,* and no one knew why. The reason became crystal clear on March 7, 1926. Less than eighteen months after her marriage to Zaharoff, the duchess died. She had been ill for several months.

Tout Va dropped its attack in the issue containing the report of the funeral, and noted that among those attending the services were Sir Basil Zaharoff, the two daughters of the deceased and M. A. Fuhrmeister, the private counselor of Prince Louis.

The newspaper returned to its attack, this time reviving the birth-certificate mystery and hinting that Zaharoff actually was a Russian Jew. But the paper was flogging a dead horse. With the death of his beloved duchess, Zaharoff no longer was interested in the throne of Monaco, nor did he have any further use for the casino. His emissaries visited banking circles and quietly informed them that Sir Basil would accept bids on his controlling interest in the casino. There were many eager bidders. Zaharoff exacted a revenge against *Tout Va* for its name-calling. He sold the controlling interest to a syndicate formed by the Paris banking house of Dreyfus and Company, a Jewish banking firm. Nor did he lose money by the sale: he sold his shares in the prospering casino for triple what he had paid for them.

Zaharoff continued to stay on at Monte Carlo after that. Although he had a large retinue, he usually was seen walking around alone; he preferred to be by himself after the death of the duchess. He was in his eighty-seventh year when he died in 1936 and was buried next to the woman he loved so long and was married to so briefly.

CHAPTER 8

The Maxwell Era

In the 1920's, the French Riviera resorts, long jealous of Monte Carlo and the visitors it was luring to the principality with its casino, started their own places. Rival gaming houses, many of them luxurious, opened in Nice, Cannes, Juan-les-Pins, Menton and Saint-Raphaël, all on the Riviera. Other resort areas, like Deauville, on the Atlantic coast and directly across the English Channel, which made it convenient for the British for brief visits, also had competing casinos.

In addition, a new revolution was taking place in Europe. The sun worshipers were coming into their own. For years, the Riviera had been almost completely a winter resort, where the wealthy, who could afford to take time off, fled from the snow and the unpleasant cold at home to the warm delights of the Côte d'Azur. Now the great middle class discovered the Riviera, not as a luxurious winter resort, but as a place to spend their summer vacations, to bask in the same magnificent sun and to be caressed by the same zephyr breezes. Fearing that the luxury hotels at the established resorts might be out of their reach, many of them poured into

Contemporary cartoon of croupiers in early days of Monte Carlo Casino surveying highway from Nice for guests approaching by carriage.

Drawing by Sem of pre-World-War-I celebrities at a Monte Carlo roulette table. In center, Baron Alphonse de Rothschild; in upper right-hand corner, Caroline Otero.

Grand Dukes Vladimir (above) and Michael of Russia *(photos from private collection)*.

Above, a rare photograph of
Edward, Prince of Wales, later
Edward VII, at thirty, when he
first visited Monte Carlo. Right,
Mrs. Lily Langtry (both photos,
W. & H. Downey, Ltd.)

Above, Feodor Chaliapin in *Boris Godunov* at Monte Carlo Opera in 1908. Below, portrait by Serov of Sergei Diaghilev, impresario of the Ballets Russes de Monte Carlo.

Above, Serge Lifar, flanked by Jean Cocteau and Darius Milhaud, with Nemtchinova after Ballets Russes performance *(photo, S. Lifar)*.

Below, young Serge Lifar with younger Pablo Picasso *(photo, S. Lifar)*.

Two exotic ladies. Above, Caroline Otero. Right, Mata Hari *(photos Musée Guimet)*.

Sir Basil Zaharoff the day he was knighted (*photo Picture Post Library*).

Two drawings of Yvette Guilbert
by Toulouse-Lautrec.

sleepy fishing villages like Antibes, Eden Roc and Cap Ferrat, and these quickly became boom towns.

This transformation occurred almost overnight. Four years earlier, Elsa Maxwell had accompanied the noted opera singer Mary Garden to the Hôtel du Parc, in Monte Carlo. It was July, and not only was the huge hotel almost deserted, but the same was true all along the Riviera. There was nothing to do except to go fishing. Friends of the singer thought she was somewhat eccentric for wanting to stay there.

As these new summer visitors began to spread out along the Riviera, they turned to the newly opened gambling casinos for recreation, but all this activity bypassed Monte Carlo. With none of the elite present at the elegant resort to gape at, the new type of visitor stayed away during the summer months, and the new competing casinos drew away former clients during the winter season.

But there was still another reason. Part of the lure of Monte Carlo prior to World War I had been the presence of the great demimondaines, such as La Belle Otero. But the war also had brought a loosening of morals. The boudoirs of some fashionable women no longer were remote to wealthy playboys who preferred women of their own class, and since they had to be more discreet at that time, they sought out quieter places. Society women were chasing professional cocottes out of business.

The result was inevitable. The queen of the gambling casinos not only was in danger of losing her crown, but business, after Zaharoff's brief ownership, had fallen off to such an extent that the Grimaldis once again were in financial difficulties, since their income was tied up so closely with the revenues the casino produced. Rumors spread that Prince Louis might give up the throne and ask that his principality be annexed by France.

The Grimaldis do not give up easily, however, and were

busy looking for ways to restore Monte Carlo to its former glory. In the previous year, 1925, Elsa Maxwell, who had built a unique career in Europe being paid to arrange parties at which millionaires and the socially elite could have real fun, had turned her talents to the Lido, of Venice, and had successfully converted this former family beach for middle-class Italians into a meeting place for the smart and sophisticated wealthy of the international set.

Prince Pierre, son-in-law of Prince Louis and father of Prince Rainier, asked Elsa to come to Monte Carlo. It was one of her few visits since the lonely summer she had spent there with Mary Garden, an indication in itself of how the resort had slipped. The prince came directly to the point: What had happened to Monte Carlo, and what could be done to restore its former popularity?

The energetic Miss Maxwell pointed out that Monte Carlo had fallen because it had failed to keep pace with the new informality that was sweeping the Riviera. The new and rising middle class might not spend as much individually as the fabulous figures who had patronized Monte Carlo before the war, but they made up for it in sheer numbers, and their patronage was valuable. The huge and gloomy casino was too stiff for them, particularly in summer, and Monte Carlo provided no place for them to swim, no beach on which to bask in the sun, despite its Sea Bathing Society name.

She bubbled with ideas. There was one short stretch of the rocky coast that could be transformed into a beach. She envisioned a new hotel directly behind it, golf links, tennis courts, a new summer casino under the stars, with a stage and dance floor. Prince Pierre weakly asked where the money would come from, but Elsa brushed this aside by telling him that to earn money you had to spend money.

Her enthusiasm was infectious, and Prince Pierre offered

her an annual fee of $6,000 to direct the transformation of Monte Carlo.

Elsa later was surprised that she had had the foresight to discuss a fee. Although she was the close friend of many enormously wealthy people and moved almost exclusively in elite circles, she had no money of her own and no urgent desire to amass it.

This woman, destined to become closely associated with the aristocracy of the twentieth century, was born in Keokuk, Iowa. Few people know that she won a baby beauty contest. In commenting on this, she made the wry remark, "May this be a warning to doting parents," and said she was a fading beauty at the age of four.

She began her career as a jazz pianist and song writer, played in a Broadway nickelodeon and went to Europe as an accompanist for revue stars. It was while she was in London that she met American heiress Dorothy Gordon; the two women became friends, and Elsa settled in England. She always had a discerning eye for talent: two of her early acquaintances were a young writer, Somerset Maugham, and a young pianist named Artur Rubinstein, and they became her lifelong friends.

Her budding career as a party giver attracted attention, and when she returned to New York in 1915 she was asked by Mrs. O. P. H. Belmont, the society leader of that era, to stage a musical for a charity to be held at the Waldorf-Astoria.

She returned to Europe after the war, and showed her disdain for money when Ralph Strassburger, an American millionaire who wanted to show his gratitude for the parties she had arranged for him in Paris, told her he had established a $5,000 credit for her at Cartier's. Elsa, who was then at Monte Carlo, asked if she could spend the money instead on Kreisler. The millionaire misunderstood and thought she was talking about a car, and offered to buy a Chrysler for her. He was incredulous when Elsa explained that she wanted the money to pay Fritz Kreisler, the great violinist, to entertain at her next party. To Elsa, talent was worth its price.

Not long after this incident, Elsa Maxwell received word that Bernard Shaw was very eager to meet her. She was flattered and pleased that the great playwright would show any interest in her. Shaw, in addition to his brilliant writing talent, was also a very shrewd and tightfisted businessman, as many producers learned. When they met, he explained that his curiosity had been aroused by a woman who would turn down diamonds to listen to a concert. Miss Maxwell laughed and asked him if he would have spent $5,000 to hear Kreisler. Shaw shook his head and replied thriftily, "For me, he would have played for nothing."

Elsa lost little time in carrying out her plans for Monte Carlo. The casino bought the land where she wanted the beach and summer hotel, and American architect Addison Mizner designed a pink stucco California-style hotel. Her first thought was to cover the pebbly beach with a tarpaulin and rubber mats, and then pour white sand over it. When tests showed that the salt water would eat the rubber, she asked a French firm instead to construct a blue-tiled swimming pool directly in front of the hotel.

While the directors of the Monte Carlo Casino may have had faith in what Elsa was doing, the contractor stared out at the blue sea, only a few steps away, and would accept the contract only after Miss Maxwell had agreed to place a clause in it that guaranteed him his full payment even if she later were proved to be of unsound mind. Elsa solemnly initialed that added clause in the contract.

The new summer casino, to be called the Sporting Club, was built only 200 yards away from the hotel. In July, 1927, the gleaming white structure was opened in a formal ceremony by King Gustaf of Sweden. Grace Moore, the singer, was the featured artist of the evening.

The casino was the first place where people could play roulette under the open sky. Not long after the opening, a 100-franc piece suddenly landed on the roulette table, bounced onto No. 8, and that number won. Actress Yvonne Printemps, who had been seated on the restaurant terrace above it and was watching the gamblers, shouted down that the coin had fallen from her purse, and asked for its return. The croupier, though, insisted upon paying her the winnings, and handed up 3,600 francs to her. Not long after this incident, a lightweight roof was placed over the tables.

Miss Maxwell remained in the employ of the casino for two years, and the socially prominent once more began to return to Monte Carlo, both in the summer and in the winter. Their presence during the summer brought the middle-class visitors along the Riviera stampeding to Monte Carlo. Their interest was not difficult to understand. During the summer of 1928, for example, the visitors to the new Monte Carlo included the Kings of Sweden, Denmark and Norway, the Crown Prince of Japan, the Maharajah of Kapurthala, the Aga Khan, the Pasha of Marrakech and such notables as Winston Churchill, Lord Curzon, Charlie Chaplin, Sacha Guitry, Maurice Chevalier and Ernst Lubitsch.

Monte Carlo returned to its place as the queen of the casinos, with a new difference. The summer season now is the busiest of all in the resort. Although Elsa Maxwell left the employ of the casino, she did not leave the resort. She instituted the system of Friday-night galas at the Sporting Club that have become social institutions on the Riviera. She usually stays on the Riviera two months every summer and often attends these galas. Her party may include as many as twenty-five guests, but she is never presented with a bill. The casino is delighted with the work of its ex-employee, and it always extends the courtesy of the house to her, except, of course, the gaming tables. Prince Rainier usually places her at his right, or at his father's right, when she attends a gala with the ruling family.

American heiresses who had married foreign titles frequently fought each other for their rightful rank at Monte Carlo. One of the wealthiest was the former Winnaretta (Winnie) Singer, daughter of the sewing machine king, Isaac Singer, who, as noted earlier, had married Prince de Polignac. Princess Winnie quarreled one day with the Duchess de La Rochefoucauld, the former Mattie Mitchell. The duchess insisted that her name was as good as the title held by the princess. "Not as a signature on a check," the wealthier woman retorted.

Despite her wealth and title, Winnie never put on an ostentatious display, and frequently wore shabby clothes. She attended one benefit in Monte Carlo where a minor clerk was accepting the donations, and when she handed him a check for 10 million francs he glanced at her clothes and handed it back, thinking it was a practical joke. Other members of the committee, aware of her identity, hurriedly accepted the check.

Elsa's old friend, Mrs. Belmont, also came to the Riviera, and quickly established herself as a leader of Monte Carlo society. Mrs. Belmont formerly had been married to W. K. Vanderbilt, and had been Miss Alva Smith, from Alabama. She had one favorite bit of advice which she gave frequently to the marriageable girls she invited to her villa: "Every woman ought to marry twice—the first time for money, the second time for love." Her daughter, Consuelo Vanderbilt, who married the Duke of Marlborough, a brother of Lord Randolph Churchill and an uncle of Winston Churchill, later gave up her title and castles, divorced the duke, and moved to a villa near Monte Carlo as the wife of a French army colonel.

One of the American women battling then to make her way into Riviera society was Mrs. Laura Corrigan, a former telephone operator and widow of a millionaire. Following Elsa Maxwell's example, she invited Kreisler to a party she was giving, but unlike Elsa, she thought she could get him to play for nothing if she invited him as a guest. The noted artist was well aware of what was being sought, and he was ready. After he had accepted the invitation, Mrs. Corrigan remarked in an offhand way that of course, he would bring his violin. Kreisler promptly replied that his fee for playing in a private home was $5,000. Since his playing was important to her plans to lure society to her party, she agreed to pay, but informed him that he could not mingle with her guests. This was the opening Kreisler was waiting for. He bowed politely and replied, "In that case I shall reduce my fee to one thousand dollars."

Swindlers discovered new ways of preying on wealthy women being attracted to the summer season at the Riviera. An aging wealthy American who did not want to face the fact that she had slipped into middle age was delighted when a dashing young Spaniard struck up a conversation with her at the Hôtel Hermitage bar. He introduced himself as Caballero Juan Ramírez del Alta del Orto di Medina. His name was long enough to sound important, even though he had invented or borrowed it. He danced attendance upon her, insisted upon escorting her everywhere, and did not even once try to kiss her hand.

He brought her to the colorful shops of Monte Carlo, and everywhere they went he offered her beautiful trinkets and rare objects. She tried to refuse at first, but he insisted with so much gallantry that she finally accepted. The sad awakening came on the morning of her departure, when she was suddenly presented with $17,000 worth of bills for the objects her escort had thrust upon her. When she said she had not bought them and told the storekeepers to take them back, she was told that they had been purchased by her through her intermediary, the caballero with the long name, who was a tourist guide. And as for taking them back, that was impossible since they already had paid the caballero his commission, 40 per cent of the purchase price.

The revitalized Monte Carlo kept up its policy of hiring the finest talent for its operas. One of the favorite performers was basso Feodor Chaliapin. This White Russian recalled the grand dukes with the reckless way he gambled, and he usually was short of cash as a result. His money demands frightened some impresarios away. "I am not only avaricious," he often said of himself, "I am downright rapacious."

He always requested a fee, even to appear at benefit performances, but he weakened once and Raoul Gunsbourg, the director of the opera, got him to agree to sing at a gala on behalf of the Monégasque Red Cross. On the morning of the show, though, Chaliapin sent the director a note saying that he was too ill to sing.

Gunsbourg, who knew Chaliapin, was not disturbed. The advance ticket sale had been large, particularly since the basso was to appear. He wrote a check for 7,000 francs and called on the singer in his hotel room. Chaliapin was in bed and enumerated the details of at least ten alarming ailments. The head of the opera commiserated with the singer, took the check out of his pocket and remarked sadly that it was too bad that the other would not be able to collect the fee.

Chaliapin grabbed the check, studied it to make sure that it was in order and announced a miraculous cure, that he would be able to sing that night after all.

Gunsbourg's productions were noted for their perfection. After a performance of *Salome,* a Middle Eastern potentate was so pleased that he wanted to decorate the director and the singing stars. He always traveled with a suitcase filled with his special decorations. Before the ceremony, his country's en-

voy, who was a personal friend of Gunsbourg, took the director aside and whispered to him that when the king passed the
case with the decoration to his chamberlain he was to push
the aide aside and request the great honor of receiving the
order directly from the hands of His Majesty.

There was a good reason for this piece of advice. The chamberlain wore a native costume with very wide sleeves, which
he used to hide cases with duplicate decorations containing
paste gems. When the king passed the genuine decoration to
him, he would use sleight of hand to switch the box. Because
of this tip, Gunsbourg was the only one to receive a decoration
that contained genuine diamonds.

Gunsbourg also told a story about a New York advertising
man, and he insisted it was true. In the opera *Otello,* the
tenor always wears dark brown make-up since the role is that
of a Negro. He said the advertising man had promised him a
large fee if he would have the tenor appear in dark make-up
in the first act, appear lighter brown in the second act, change
the color to yellow in the third, and finally appear in his natural complexion in the last act, at which point two stagehands
would lower a streamer carrying the name of a well-known
soap. None of Gunsbourg's listeners were ever able to decide
whether somebody had tried to pull the director's leg or he
was doing it to his listeners.

As part of the casino's new look, René Léon, its director,
brought American show girls to Monte Carlo; not only did
they score a hit on the stage, but many of them made very successful marriages. The lovely Xandra Rambeau married a son
of William Randolph Hearst's, and blonde Betty Sundmark
became the wife of Argentine millionaire Albert Dodero.

One of these girls was Evelyn Crowell, who wanted to get
an even sun tan and had stretched out on the balcony of her
room at the Hôtel de Paris, after carefully draping a towel
across it to protect herself from Peeping Toms. She was rest-

ing with her eyes closed when she heard a typical American whistle of admiration from below. A vagrant breeze had whipped part of the towel away. She hastily wrapped the towel around her and indignantly called down to the man below, "I see you are no gentleman." Her anger evaporated into involuntary laughter when he called back, "I see you are no gentleman, either." The man was wealthy Day Elliot, and not long afterward the couple were married.

The Dolly Sisters were one of the best-known dancing teams of that era. Jenny entered the casino one night with Gordon Selfridge, the London department-store heir, and they sat down at a baccarat table where the players included the Aga Khan, the former King of Portugal and Hungarian Prince Esterházy.

Jenny had an exceptional run of luck, and the other players gradually dropped out. Losses and winnings at baccarat can run very high. In most cases the casino does not run the bank, but takes a cut on the play. The banker and one player face each other while the others at the table can bet on the cards. Just two were now at the table, Prince Esterházy, who held the bank, and Jenny. She had a pile of chips worth almost 10 million francs in front of her and staked it all at once. The others were surprised since she usually was a levelheaded person. The bet obviously was in the nature of a dare, and the Hungarian nobleman accepted the challenge. Jenny won, and she continued playing until Prince Esterházy had lost 15 million francs and gave up.

"I am glad I defeated Prince Esterházy," she said triumphantly. "My grandfather was a serf on his family's estate and used to be whipped by the overseer."

Cole Porter, the noted song writer, was a persistent enemy of snobs on the Riviera. Although he made a great deal of money from his successful Broadway shows, he also had substantial wealth from inherited mines and forests in Virginia.

To show up the snobs, he invented a very rich American couple, Mr. and Mrs. S. L. Fitch, from Muskogee, Oklahoma, and then sent in notes about them to the Riviera column of the Paris edition of the New York *Herald*. He always had the Fitches being entertained by royalty, or going off on brief lion hunts with maharajahs. They never seemed to mingle with such common people as millionaires, and hostesses along the Riviera were frantic trying to snare the Fitches for their own parties. No one knew where they were staying. One brazen young impostor was treated as a social lion himself because he claimed to know the Fitches, and was showered with invitations. Porter carried on his campaign for six months, until Hearst society columnist Cholly Knickerbocker printed the truth.

Like Cole Porter, Gunsbourg, the opera director, also heartily disliked snobs, and when he met one he would repeat the story of the banker Cahen, of Antwerp, who had legally adopted the name of Cahen d'Anvers. In time he began signing his letters, "C. d'Anvers." One day while in Monte Carlo he mailed a post card to an old friend, using that signature. His friend was a banker named Oppenheim, who lived in Cologne. Oppenheim promptly sent his friend a reply: "Thanks for your greetings. Hope you are having a nice vacation." It was signed, "O. de Cologne."

Not all the famous parties were given by Elsa Maxwell. Grace Moore gave an outdoor farewell supper for her fiancé, Chato Elizaga, on the grounds of the Hôtel du Cap. Among the guests were Alexander Woollcott and the Scott Fitzgeralds. After a great many farewell toasts, Zelda Fitzgerald climbed on a table, stepped out of the black lace panties she wore under her evening gown and solemnly presented them to the guest of honor as a farewell gift. To show his appreciation, Elizaga jumped into the water wearing his full-dress suit. Woollcott brought the party to a close when he stripped naked, put on his straw hat, lit a cigar, strolled back to the lobby and asked the baffled porter for his room key.

Hotel men in Monte Carlo learned to be prepared for anything. A Viennese steel man ordered a champagne bath for a young lady he had met ten minutes earlier, and a well-known British actor telephoned the desk clerk at 3 A.M. and requested that the 12-girl chorus line of can-can dancers from Maxim's night club be sent up to his suite. An Italian royal prince locked himself in his room early one evening and left orders he was not to be disturbed. When the maid entered the room the next morning, all the furniture in the suite had been sawed into little pieces. "Put it on my bill," he directed.

A wealthy South American had a secret yearning to go on an underwater trip in a submarine, and asked André Sella, the owner of the hotel where he was staying, if he knew where he could rent one. The hotel man knew a submarine commander whose unit was stationed in nearby Villefranche. The officer, risking court-martial, entered into the spirit of the joke, and at dawn the next day, the millionaire was smuggled aboard and the boat cruised around underwater all morning. When the elated South American returned to the hotel that afternoon, he drew out his checkbook and asked the price. The hotel owner lifted both hands in protest and with a dead-pan face replied, "The submarine belongs to our hotel fleet. It is at our clients' disposal."

Gabrielle (Coco) Chanel, the famous fashion designer and perfume maker, spent most of her time during the 1920's in a 40-room villa on the outskirts of Monte Carlo, where she stayed with the Duke of Westminster, whose family owns great chunks of the city of London. The two gambled frequently at the casino and held many parties in the port of Monte Carlo, aboard the yacht they used.

Chanel returned to Paris twice each year to prepare her

fashion collections, to the great distress of the duke, who always urged her to marry him. But nothing could induce Coco to give up her ateliers in the Rue Cambon. "There are already twenty duchesses in England," she told him, "but there is only one Chanel."

The great love of her life had been another Englishman, Arthur Capel, the owner of many coal mines. He had met her at the Pau Hunt, an annual event of pre-World War I Anglo-American socialites in France. He installed her in a town house on the Avenue Gabriel and introduced her to Paris café society. She lived in Deauville during the war and started copying from the French sailors the heavy sweaters and wool jackets that were to revolutionize the fashion world and make her famous. It was largely due to Chanel that women discarded the enveloping laced-up corsets. Capel died after the war in an automobile accident.

When the White Russian refugees poured into Paris, she hired many of them as seamstresses and salesmen, and made Grand Duke Dimitri her public relations director. She also helped finance the ballet of Diaghilev.

She created her famous perfume, Chanel No. 5, in 1922, and it earned her so much money in three years that she was able to buy the Louzon Palace, in Paris, and become one of the great hostesses of the city. It was at that time that she met the Duke of Westminster.

Almost everything she did created fashion news. While she was preparing to go to the Monte Carlo Opera one evening, the water heater in her bathroom exploded and singed her beautiful dark hair. Coco promptly cut her hair short. Her entrance at the opera that night caused a sensation, and started the vogue for bobbed hair. During the 1930's, Chanel fell in love with fashion designer Paul Iribe. When he died of a heart attack during a tennis match, she became melancholy and finally closed her famous fashion house shortly before World War II. She remained in retirement for fifteen years, living on the income from her perfume sales. Her friends finally persuaded her to reopen her ateliers in 1954, and now, at almost eighty, Coco Chanel again is one of the leading clothes designers in Paris. At this writing she still divides her time between her shop in the Rue Cambon and her Monte Carlo villa. During the summer of 1962, Alan Lerner, the co-author of *My Fair Lady,* was visiting her, gathering material to write a musical comedy about her life. "Why not a musical tragedy?" she asked him.

One man's name for many years was synonymous in the public's mind with that of Monte Carlo, that of the earlier mentioned E. Phillips Oppenheim, the writer. Many of his novels had a Monte Carlo background, and he had millions of readers all over the world. His background material was authentic; he lived permanently on the Riviera from 1923 until his death, in 1946, with the exception of the war years. In many ways he was as much a character in Monte Carlo as those he created.

He first visited the resort during the winter season in 1895, when the Prince of Wales and his friends ran the Riviera. He was fascinated by the wealthy society there and was determined to become rich enough to take part in it. Many of his books were serialized in *The Saturday Evening Post, Collier's* and other magazines, and he earned large sums. He went to the casino almost every day, where he won and lost fortunes. He lived in a villa at Cagnes with his wife, a cook, a valet and a chauffeur, and he also owned a yacht.

In one of his books he made the mistake of describing a so-called infallible system of winning at roulette. Some of his readers, forgetting that his book was fiction, went to Monte Carlo and complained bitterly when they lost. "Oppy," as he was known along the Riviera, did not want to lose face, and staunchly upheld the system he had described. A group of irate readers accompanied him to the casino, where he was going to show them how to break the bank. By dawn his savings had been wiped out. He had to sell his yacht to raise enough money to pay his debts, and he hurried to New York to talk his publisher into giving him a good-sized advance.

His fiction probably reached the height of its popularity during the depression, when his stories of dazzling social life on the Riviera provided escape literature. He often referred to the depression years as "those splendid prosperous days."

The Sporting Club became one of his favorite places. He held many parties there, and never seemed to mind gate-crashers who placed their drinks on his bill.

One of his close friends was American-born Anita Stewart, widow of the Duke of Braganza, the heir to the Portuguese throne, who renounced his rights to it after his father had been dethroned.

The duchess was poor and lived in London in an attic room in the Ritz Hotel, but she was widely entertained on the Riviera, where she went every season. She regularly visited her husband's embalmed corpse, and then would entertain Monte Carlo society with vivid descriptions of his appearance. At one time she complained that his left cheek had turned green. She also said that his beard had been growing with great luxuriance, and seemed genuinely delighted at this sign of posthumous vitality.

Almost anything that happened in Monte Carlo was grist for Oppenheim's books. A swindler, posing as a Biarritz industrialist, entered a fashionable jewelry store in Monte Carlo and selected a diamond necklace priced at 550,000 francs. He offered a check on a bank in Bordeaux, and the jeweler asked if he could verify the check by telephoning the bank. The customer agreed. The call was made, and the jeweler was assured that the man was one of the bank's best clients, that such a check was a mere trifle for him. Three days later the check came back from the Bordeaux bank with the notation that the signer had no account there.

Police finally solved the mystery. The swindler had worked with two accomplices, a man and a woman. They were waiting in a flower shop opposite the jewelry store and saw the jeweler place the call to Bordeaux. This was a trunk call that would take time to put through. While waiting, the merchant returned to chat with his customer. Meanwhile, the accomplices canceled the call, waited for several minutes and telephoned the jeweler, with the girl posing as the bank secretary. She then put her companion on the phone, and he posed as the bank manager. The thieves were caught when they tried to pull the same trick again. Oppenheim used this incident in one of his novels.

One of his favorite stories involved an American woman whom he discreetly called Princess Ravioli. She had married a waiter and obtained false papers that made him a prince, but he could not quite live up to the part. They entered the Monte Carlo Opera one night, and he was wearing a full-dress suit resplendent with decorations. He paused at the threshold, carefully doused his cigarette and then placed it behind his ear to save it for after the show. The marriage fell apart when he won a large sum one night at the casino and left his princess flat, never even returning to his room to get his clothes. He was never seen in Monte Carlo again.

Oppenheim was a close friend of King Gustaf V of Sweden, and of Professor Voronoff, who was known for his rejuvenation operations. Oppenheim was a man of sixty when he noticed a beautiful blonde on the beach of La Garoupe while he was on his yacht, dictating a story. He disembarked, was seen starting with the lady in the direction of Monte Carlo and did not return to his yacht until ten days later, when he resumed his dictation.

Monte Carlo continued its merry pace during the years

leading to World War II. Mr. Sella, the owner of the nearby Hôtel du Cap, received a wire from Henry Morgenthau, United States Secretary of the Treasury, requesting him to reserve a suite for ten days. The hotel was full, and the owner sent a reply of regret, but Morgenthau already was under way from Paris. He arrived at 1 A.M. and asked for his room.

Since Morgenthau was an old customer, the hotel owner had to find space for him, and finally decided to give him a suite occupied by an elderly Englishwoman who habitually took sleeping pills that would keep her slumbering soundly through the night. She was placed on a stretcher and transported, along with her baggage, to a neighboring villa owned by Sella.

When the woman awoke the next morning, she stared at the unfamiliar room, and then hurried to the window. Instead of looking out upon the sea, she saw sheep grazing in a field. The frightened woman ran screaming out into the street in her night clothes. She left that night for London. Morgenthau did not know that the woman had been dispossessed to make room for him.

By a strange quirk of fate, the last big party before the war was held by Elsa Maxwell. A Canadian friend, Eleanor Loder, had bequeathed her lifetime possession of a beautiful 10-room villa with a terrace overlooking the Riviera coast. She received this gift on August 24, 1939, the day after the Hitler-Stalin pact. She promptly invited 200 people to attend a housewarming party at the villa on August 31.

It was a busy week of preparation for Elsa, and she had no time to read the papers. Cleaning women had to be hired to scrub the floors and wash the curtains, while she hunted through the art shops of Cannes and Monaco for furniture. Her guests did arrive, many of them with packed luggage, and Elsa learned that Europe was on the brink of another war. Most of the guests talked about the crisis, and the cocktails and sandwiches were left largely untouched. About 9 P.M., Elsa telephoned her long-time friend Joseph P. Kennedy, the American ambassador in London. When he learned that she still was on the Riviera, he urged her to take the next ship home. "It is just a question of hours," he told her.

Elsa later described what happened after she had replaced the receiver:

"We went out on the terrace. The night was warm, and the coast glittered under the cloudless sky. Suddenly a black carpet rolled from the west over Cannes and put out all the lights in the houses and in the streets. Below us, Golfe-Juan and Antibes were thrown into darkness as if by two giant hands. And then the reflection of the light slowly faded between Nice and Monte Carlo."

France had had her first air-raid blackout. The war was on, and another era had come to a close at Monte Carlo.

CHAPTER 9

Business As Usual

The roulette wheels of the Monte Carlo Casino never stopped spinning during World War II. They spun less frequently during the first year, when patrons were scarce and consisted largely of expatriates, most of whom were English or American. The casino lost five million francs that year, not because the gamblers were lucky, but because not enough money was played to cover the high overhead. But with the fall of France and the occupation of Monaco, first by the Italians and then by the Nazis, the tempo quickened, the wheels whirled day and night, and the profits of the casino rose to dizzying heights, the largest in its history up to that time.

When Hitler ordered the invasion of Poland, signaling the start of the war, Prince Louis followed the path set by his father in 1914, and hoped that his principality could sit it out as a proclaimed neutral. Meanwhile, Prince Rainier, the heir to the throne, joined the French Army.

Monaco's bid for neutrality was of great importance to the expatriates, who since 1919 had come in ever increasing numbers to Monte Carlo and the neighboring areas of the Ri-

viera. These self-exiles were divided into two extremes. At
one end were the enormously wealthy, the socially prominent
and members of the international set. These included such
figures as Mrs. Laura Corrigan, of Cleveland, the Duke of
Windsor and the Aga Khan. The great majority, though,
were at the other extreme, which was composed largely of
elderly English spinsters living on fixed modest annuities or
pensions, who had been caught at home in a financial
squeeze of rising prices and no way to increase their incomes.
These "foolish virgins," as a novelist later described them,
discovered that if they bypassed the luxury hotels and villas
they could live on the Riviera in greater comfort and much
cheaper than at home. It was possible during most of the
period between the two great wars to get by on little more
than a dollar a day, if absolutely necessary. At the start
of World War II there were more than 30,000 British nationals residing permanently on the Riviera and about 3,000
Americans.

It was the smaller group of millionaires and playboys
about whom one read in the newspapers before the war;
little people seldom make news anywhere, and one of the
chief hostesses of that era was the earlier mentioned Mrs.
Laura Corrigan, a former Cleveland telephone operator who
had married a millionaire and was widowed several years
later, inheriting some 80 million dollars to help assuage her
grief.

Unable to crash the rigid society of Cleveland after her
husband's death, Laura came to the Riviera, where she
opened a sumptuous villa and also maintained a lavish apartment in the Hôtel de Paris. Many people laughed at her at
first because of her pretensions. When she mentioned that
she was going on a cruise to the Greek islands, she was urged
to visit a certain sight. Knowing nothing whatever about the
classic historical ruins that dot Greece, she assumed that she

was being urged to visit socially important people. "They invited me," she told her startled guest, "but I haven't the time to stay with them."

But the persevering widow continued her party-throwing and did become one of the great hostesses on the Côte d'Azur and in London. For one party she chartered an ocean liner for a month, transformed it into a private yacht and invited hundreds of friends for a lengthy cruise. When the month was over, she had to spend additional thousands of dollars removing all the expensive fittings she had installed because the contract required that the ship be returned in its original condition. During the London season she often rented the palace of the Duke of Marlborough and was hostess to royalty, including the Duke and Duchess of Kent.

Though most of the expatriates did leave the Riviera at the outbreak of the war, many thousands continued to remain in or near Monte Carlo, hopeful that Monaco's neutrality shield would protect them. The tiny principality also became a haven for many Jews fleeing from the Nazis as their homelands were overrun. The brittle and uneasy laughter of the reduced number of patrons in the casino was a painful sound. Panic broke out after the fall of Paris, when Mussolini bravely ordered his troops to advance on the French outposts at nearby Menton.

In the midst of a total war, with every ship badly needed, Winston Churchill had to send vessels to Monte Carlo to evacuate the British nationals who had remained on the Riviera. All he could spare were two tiny, rusty and dirty coal-carrying colliers, and more than 1,500 people, including Somerset Maugham, were crammed into these small vessels. Not all who wanted to go were able to board them, and others elected to stay. The boats were so overcrowded that their strained engines could make little headway against tides and it required almost two weeks for these ships to reach England. Many of the wealthy were able to make their way across the Spanish border and then return home. Laura Corrigan, though, moved in the opposite direction. The United States still was not at war, and she went to Paris, where she turned her energies toward helping French prisoners of war. She sold all her jewels to raise funds for these activities and remained in Paris for the duration. After the liberation, in 1944, the former social butterfly was made a Commander of the Legion of Honor by a grateful French Government. She died four years later in New York.

Italian troops were the first to march into Monte Carlo, ignoring the protests of Monaco's Minister of the Interior. Some residents of Italian ancestry welcomed the troops by waving green-white-and-red flags, and the small principality also developed its own quisling. A former Minister of Finance hatched a plot to arrest Prince Louis and other prominent Monégasques and have the independent state annexed by Italy.

Prince Louis was informed of the scheme, and ordered the arrest of the conspirators. The occupation authorities forced their release, but Mussolini informed them that he had not entered the war to conquer Monte Carlo.

All English nationals under seventy years of age were rounded up and interned at Camp Sospel. One of the inmates was Mrs. Fox, of Scotland, who gallantly lied about her age. When occupation authorities learned that she was over eighty, they released her, but the Scotswoman refused to admit her age and they had great difficulty in liberating her.

"A real scandal," she shouted at them. "What has happened to Italian chivalry?"

Occupation troops met their match in Miss Amy Paget. All during the war she defiantly flew the Union Jack at her château, Garibondy. She was almost ninety, and the peppery little woman planted herself in front of the flagpole whenever officers came up and demanded the flag be taken down. "My home is my castle," she told them. Since the only way to lower the flag would have required manhandling the frail, aged woman, the baffled officers left and finally pretended the flag was not there.

Monaco raises very little of its own food, and prices soon skyrocketed. Many of the elderly exiles were kept alive by food packages given to them by friendly croupiers and other casino employees, who were basking in unexpected prosperity.

With the fall of France, Monte Carlo became the favorite playground for a combination of French collaborators, German and Italian businessmen, Nazi officers on leave, and such adventurers of uncertain origins as always manage to profit from war. Between 1940 and 1942, more than 200 new holding companies were registered in Monaco. Many of these are believed to have been fronts for such leading Nazis as Goering and Himmler, who were using the companies to smuggle to Switzerland and other neutral areas the treasures they had been looting. Other firms were owned by Frenchmen trying to hide the millions they made as purveyors to the occupation powers. Many of these visitors gambled as if there would be no tomorrow. They made huge bets, did not seem to mind their losses and stuffed large bank notes into the box for the croupiers. From a loss of five million francs during the first year of the war, the figures after the occupation tell their own story: In 1941, the casino made a profit of six million francs; the net rose sharply to 28 million in 1942, and then zoomed to 106 million for the next two years.

One of the oddest personalities who appeared in Monte Carlo shortly after the occupation was Michel Skolnikoff, a fat, bald man, said to have been born in Rumania, who, although believed to have been Jewish, was employed by the

Nazis to run a black market network that supplied Hitler's army with strategic materials that the Allied blockade was trying to keep out of Germany. He seemed to be able to obtain anything: ammonia, ball bearings, tents, bags of sugar; nothing seemed beyond his reach.

He became one of the largest property holders in Monte Carlo and spent more than 450 million francs buying up hotels, apartment houses, châteaux, virtually any property that he could find for sale.

After he had amassed his first billion francs, he gave an elaborate party at the Hôtel de Paris for thirty-six people, including dignitaries from the Vichy government. The food, supplied by Skolnikoff, included delicacies that the chefs at the hotel had not seen since the start of the war.

These revels were taking place almost within sight and sound of Allied fliers being held in a prisoner-of-war camp at Fort de la Revere, in the hills in back of Monaco. More than 1,000 pilots were confined there, including Captain Whitney Straight, of the Royal Air Force, a wealthy sportsman, who had been a frequent visitor to Monte Carlo before the war.

Like most of the prisoners, he was busy prowling the compound, looking for weak points and hoping to escape. Because he knew the region and had friends in Monte Carlo, he felt he had a good chance of avoiding capture if he managed to get away. He finally found what he was looking for, an abandoned and forgotten water main. The camp was on a hill near La Turbie. He knew there was a small stream at the foot of the hill and reasoned that the old main probably had run down to that stream. Since the pipe was forty inches in diameter, a man could wriggle through it. He did not know whether the pipe was clear on the outside; help would be needed to check that.

Since taking the pipe route was too risky without knowing where it ended, the resourceful captain set about to make his own escape. He had been wounded when his plane was shot down, and by feigning that his injuries were causing him severe pain he induced the camp physician to transfer him to a military hospital in Nice. Once there, Captain Straight palmed the sleeping pills the nurse gave him, managed to slip them into his guard's drink, and fled the hospital when the other fell asleep. He kept to the hills and worked his way undetected to the Scotch Teahouse, on Boulevard des Moulins, in Monte Carlo, which, despite its name, was operated by a Frenchwoman, Mme. Tranchard. Straight had patronized the restaurant before the war. The woman gave him refuge, and the Monégasque underground, headed by a British naval officer, provided Straight with false identity papers. Before leaving for the Nice hospital, the British pilot had made a bet with several of his fellow prisoners that he would be playing in the Monte Carlo Casino within three weeks. He was well ahead of his schedule when he daringly entered the casino. He played there several times while arrangements were completed to get him to England. Although he was recognized by some of the casino employees, none of them gave him away.

Straight told the underground leader about the abandoned water main, and American O.S.S. agent Val Williams, who had been parachuted into the region several months before to build up a resistance network along the Riviera, led a group of local men to examine the pipe. They found it usable. The exit was carefully screened by underbrush, a route established leading to the Scotch Teahouse and a chain of contacts set up to ship the escaping pilots to England. A Polish priest who visited the prison camp each Sunday to conduct Mass acted as go-between, carrying messages to R.A.F. pilot Truffy Higginson, the senior officer of the prisoners. While unsuspecting Italian guards patrolled the camp, a tunnel was dug from one of the barracks to the pipe. It was

completed within a month, and Higginson led six of his men
to a successful escape. Even after the war, Mme. Tranchard
was still puzzled by the actions of several of the first escapees.
She had great difficulty keeping them away from the Monte
Carlo Casino. "They said they needed money to pay a bet,"
she exclaimed.

With the first successful escape, the water main became a
magnificent pipeline to freedom. Within a period of several
months, 242 badly needed pilots escaped from the camp, and
only fourteen failed to make it back to England. On one
night alone, thirty-five men fled. One other had to stay behind; he was too stout, got stuck shortly after entering the
pipe, and was hauled back into the barracks. British submarines were maintaining an almost steady schedule, meeting escapees at lonely beaches and ferrying them back to
England.

The baffled Italian guards were unable to find the tunnel,
and the occupation force became so jittery they began arrest-
ing every civilian in Monte Carlo who looked at all suspicious to them. None of the escapees were picked up that way.

On November 11, 1942, as a result of Allied landings in
North Africa, the Nazis spread throughout unoccupied
France, and by agreement with Mussolini, this included the
Riviera. A section of the Gestapo was the first German unit
to enter Monte Carlo, and immediately took over the Hôtel
de Paris. Several days later General von Kohlermann arrived
with his Panzer division. He was unhappy that the Gestapo
had requisitioned the best hotel, and tried unsuccessfully to
get them to move out. He then wanted to take over the
Hôtel Hermitage, but the personnel there had strewn rubble
in all salons and bedrooms to have this beautiful hotel clas-
sified as "uninhabitable for German troops." He finally settled at the Hôtel Métropole and set up his command unit at
the Villa Eleanor.

Technically, Germany was not at war with Monaco, and the Gestapo could not operate in its usual highhanded fashion. The Italians had not molested the Jews and other refugees in Monte Carlo, and even gave advance notice when they learned that the Gestapo were coming. Prince Louis placed as many as he could in the different houses and estates he owned along the Riviera, and many Monégasques followed his example. The Gestapo let the French S.S. do their dirty work. While they organized the raids, it was the collaborators who actually carried them out. Every few weeks these sorties were conducted in different sections of Monaco and every house was searched from roof to basement.

These raids usually lasted thirty-six hours, and after that those who were still free could reappear and would be in no danger until the next period. If Police Chief Conan, of the Monaco Sûreté, received word in time, he quickly passed the information to the section slated to be searched. Even where the S.S. men had flushed out some prey, Prince Louis frequently succeeded in preventing them from being deported.

General von Kohlermann, who did not like the Gestapo, also proved to be an unexpected ally, and would maneuver his troops to hamper the work of the agents.

The casino operated unhindered; in fact, it was treated as if it were sacrosanct. Every night, a small German military plane flew low over Monaco to make certain that the blackout rules were being observed, and hand grenades were thrown wherever a light was seen. But the plane always made a wide circle of the casino to make certain that no grenade would fall on it by accident.

In the fall of 1943, when copper and other metals became desperately short in Germany, the Gestapo suggested to General von Kohlermann that he remove the casino's heavy Moorish roof, made of the finest copper, and have it sent to the Fatherland. The general, who was a great casino fan, not only refused but succeeded in having the Monte Carlo Casino officially declared "a cultural and historical monument," and therefore untouchable, the only gambling casino ever to receive that distinction.

When on August 14, 1944, Allied troops landed between Saint-Tropez and Saint-Raphaël, Monégasques celebrated because they expected the 7th Army to move along the coast toward the Italian border. Their joy was short-lived; the troops, instead, slashed up the Rhone Valley toward Lyons, leaving the Riviera for later mop-up action. Instead, planes bombed all the roads and bridges between Fréjus and Monaco, and also raided the Monte Carlo harbor and sank seven mine sweepers. They also scored a direct hit on the command headquarters. These bombings cut off the already meager food supply, and rations were set up, with one pint of soup a day allotted to each inhabitant. Hotels prepared the food and distributed it.

At the end of the month several armored columns under the command of General Robert T. Frederick finally began moving up the Riviera coast. Nice surrendered without a fight, and when this news reached Monte Carlo the German staff officers quickly packed, paid their bills and headed for the nearby Italian border. They left 300 soldiers in the fortress of Mont-Agel, above Monaco, but after a warship moved into position and lobbed a few shells into the fort the soldiers surrendered.

Skolnikoff left well ahead of the German officers and headed for Spain. He was supposed to have left with a fortune in jewels and gold. He did get across the border, with French resistance men in pursuit. His mutilated body later was found in a field.

The first American soldiers rolled into Monaco on September 3. The lead jeep stopped at the Place d'Armes. Two G.I.'s stared at the beautiful luxury hotels, the lush, blooming gardens, and then called out, "Hey, Bud, where are we?"

But some of the men in the following cars did not have to be told. Several of them drove up the hill of Monte Carlo, leaped out of their vehicles, raced up the marble steps of the casino and greeted the porter, "Hello, Gaston, we're back again."

Before they could enter the casino, one of the directors hurried out. "Not in uniform, gentlemen," he said. "Not in uniform. Please find civilian clothes." Not even the liberation of Monaco could cause the casino to relax the no· uniform rule, but the director did promise to keep the casino open until 4 A.M.

With the help of hundreds of happy Monégasques, a strangely clad group of G.I.'s descended on the *salons privés* that night; it didn't matter that their clothes did not fit or that they looked like a tatterdemalion crew; they were in civilian dress and were royally welcomed to the casino. For many of them it was their first introduction to roulette and baccarat. There were no dice tables then, and there are still no poker games in the casino.

The next morning, the cleanup began in Monaco. Barbed wire strung by the Nazis was removed and more than 600 hidden mines were found along the small coastline. The principality promptly expelled all those residents who had welcomed the Italian troops four years earlier, and some of the businessmen who had collaborated with the Nazis and did not get away were turned over to the Allies.

General Frederick, then the youngest two-star general in the American Army, wanted to turn Monaco into a leave center for G.I.'s and set up canteens, clubs and PX shops for 12,000 men. Prince Louis pointed out that there was not

enough room in his tiny principality for so many men plus
the regular visitors who would be returning. He wanted to
limit it to 1,200 men, all officers.

He soon had his answer. The general was very popular
with his troops because he had sloughed with them in the
front lines all during the Italian campaign. He promptly
announced that Monaco was off limits for all Allied personnel, regardless of rank. Within one week after Monaco had
been liberated, it had been completely evacuated of troops
as well. Not a soldier was seen in it.

Even General Eisenhower obeyed the order. In the summer of 1945, he arrived on the Riviera for a few days' rest
and stayed at Eden Roc, near Monte Carlo, but on French
soil. After V-E Day, German prisoners had removed the
mines hidden on the hotel grounds, and pigs had been run
over its parklike setting to set off any explosives that might
have been overlooked. The grounds were considered mine-
free when Ike arrived.

Several times daily he walked through the park and sat
down under a large palm tree facing the sea. He scrupulously
obeyed the off-limits order, did not go near the casino, preferring the serenity under his favorite tree. His vacation
passed without incident.

Several months later the owner of Eden Roc received from
the Allied Military Document Center in Berlin a German
map showing the location of all the mines buried on the
grounds of his hotel.

He slowly checked them off against those removed and
then stared, aghast. One bomb, a huge 200-pound one, still
remained. Workmen were summoned, and cautiously dug
around the spot until they did unearth the bomb. It was
right at the foot of General Eisenhower's favorite tree.

CHAPTER 10

Sharpshooters and Freebooters

Although Hollywood star Edward G. Robinson may not know it, it was a remark he made that finally resulted in the introduction of the American gambling game *le crap* at the Monte Carlo Casino. And of course, it is not his fault that in addition to legitimate visitors, the dice games brought sharpshooters looking for an angle, a crooked way to beat the house. Robinson had spent an evening playing roulette and got bored with watching the bobbing white ball. As he left, he remarked to a companion, "Hell, I would give anything right now for a real crap game."

The casino maintains a staff of men who mingle unobtrusively with the guests, watching everything that goes on and keeping their ears open for conversational tidbits that might help the management improve service. The Hollywood actor's remarks were overheard and duly appeared on the desk of the directors.

Other Americans had spoken wistfully of shooting craps, and when a movie star with ample funds voiced the same thought this was enough to make casino officials take notice. Chief croupier Louis Delamare was sent to the United States to check on the feasibility of adding dice games to the casino's gambling choices. He visited casinos in Nevada, the only state where gambling is legal, and possibly a few of the well-known high-class rug joints that somehow manage to operate without great benefit of secrecy in other sections of the country. Although Delamare may have had some diffi- culty in understanding why well-dressed men, who obvi- ously had money, were pleading that baby needed a new pair of shoes, he did grasp the incredible speed with which gam- blers could lose money at the dice tables—it is the fastest of all gambling games—and on his return he recommended that the casino depart from tradition and convert one of the *salons privés* to the American game of craps.

Several months later the first dice tables were installed in the Salle Schmidt, a salon with thick mahogany walls, which would help muffle the shouted incantations that Delamare explained always seemed to accompany dice games. As a further homey touch for Americans, one-armed bandits, slot machines, were placed in the casino lobby.

To the happy surprise of officials, the dice tables not only attracted American tourists, but became popular with visi- tors from all over the world, including Europeans, and soon became one of the major sources of revenue for the casino. Delamare's trip had been a most profitable one for Monte Carlo.

Experienced in the way of crooks, the casino took ample precautions to protect itself. It employed the same reputable Reno firm that manufactures tamper-proof dice for many of the leading legal casinos in the United States, and special dice were designed for them. These were made of transpar- ent plastic in exclusive shades of green and red, reserved just for its use, with the inscription *Monte Carlo* engraved on the dice.

But the introduction of craps at Monte Carlo sounded the clarion call for the easy-money boys. How many hurried

Mrs. William Kissam Vanderbilt, Jr. *(private collection).*

Portrait by Porter of Mrs. O. H. P. Belmont, society leader and mother of Consuelo Vanderbilt.

Consuelo Vanderbilt—painting by Clemente del Camino.

Scott and Zelda Fitzgerald in front of their Riviera summer villa, 1929
(*photo, private collection*).

Gabrielle Chanel in 1929 (*photo, private collection*).

Inset, drawing of Chanel by Dorian.

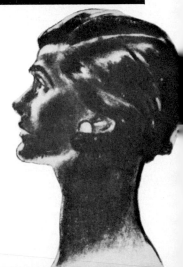

The beach at Monte Carlo *(photo Maison de Monaco)*.

Elsa Maxwell talking with Jack Warner at Monte Carlo dinner table
(*photo De Sazo-Manciet*).

Sir Bernard and Lady Docker and her son in Monte Carlo (*photo De Sazo-Manciet*).

Ex-King Farouk *(photo AGIP)*.

Tony and Sarah Churchill Beauchamp *(photo BBC)*.

there to look the situation over is unknown, of course, but it is known that it did arouse the hunting instincts of three Americans, two of whom had minor police records. The trio were Jason Lee, born in Korea; Arif Shaker, a Lebanese; and Philip Aggie, an Irishman, all American citizens. Lee and Aggie had police records.

At that time Lee was running a Western-style night club in Tokyo, and he became the scout for others, flying to Monte Carlo to examine the dice-table setup and to probe for flaws. He soon thought he had spotted one in the operations of Salle Schmidt.

Lee was familiar with American gambling places, particularly the so-called sawdust joints, which are illegally operated gambling clubs that do not go in for plush surroundings. At many of these places the players either are in their shirt sleeves or have their sleeves rolled back. This is not to give them more freedom for action, as the casual observer might think, but is intended to prevent the oldest trick of all in dice games, the sleight-of-hand introduction of a pair of loaded dice that can be hidden up a sleeve. Those who do wear jackets are watched closely by the stickmen at the tables.

Shirt sleeves are frowned upon at dignified Monte Carlo, and it would be unseemly to ask the type of patron there to roll back his sleeves. Lee realized that a crowded table could afford an opportunity to switch dice. He managed to palm a discarded pair and cautiously flew to Tangiers before shipping the dice to his associates in Los Angeles. They steered clear of the reputable Reno firm and hired a manufacturer in California to copy the official Monte Carlo dice, with certain omissions on various pairs.

On February 19, 1956, all three arrived at Monte Carlo to put their plan into operation. Lee was to be the man who handled and switched the dice, and his bets would not be too large; his companions would be placing the heavy bets. Many players do not roll the dice themselves, but place bets on the throws made by others. Their first day was a Sunday, and they played it straight, even making a few sucker bets, and lost money, hoping to impress on the croupiers that they were just ordinary tourists.

The next morning, they got down to business, bet consistently on a few numbers and soon were $17,500 ahead. In addition, Lee would go off on a sensational winning streak, during which he would toss nothing but a 7 on his first throws. Though players do get hot streaks and will throw winning combinations time after time, these usually include rolling for a point and not a steady barrage of naturals. The inspector at the table casually reached over, took the dice and handed a new pair to Lee, who soon lost his turn. He and Shaker hurried back to their hotel, packed their luggage and took a taxi to the Nice airport. Aggie remained behind as a decoy.

The inspector slipped the pair he had taken to an attendant, who brought them to the director's office, where they were immediately compared with an official set. The Los Angeles manufacturer had been unable to duplicate exactly the special green color used by the casino. They were slightly darker. In addition, they were one millimeter smaller and two milligrams heavier. This particular pair had been loaded to throw 7's forever.

Monaco police had no difficulty tracing Lee and Shaker, and they were arrested at the airport. Aggie was picked up at the Casino. A search of their luggage turned up 164 pairs of counterfeit Monte Carlo dice, some hidden in long woolen hose. Some were loaded to produce only 7's; on others the number 2, 3 or 5 was missing. Lee had been switching the dice in use on the table to his own pairs, which were designed to favor the appearance of certain numbers more often than any others, and the gang would bet heavily whenever the switch was made. He had become overconfident when he introduced a loaded pair that produced 7 only. Delamare had received a thorough course of instruction on dice switching during his visit to the United States, and he had coached his men well. All three members of the gang were convicted and sent to prison. Prince Rainier later ordered them deported.

As a further precaution after this episode, the dice used at the casino were redesigned to include secret markings that enable house men to tell at a glance whether they are genuine. The colors now in use are water-green, blood-red and purple.

In its hundred years of existence, the Monte Carlo Casino has been the target of thousands of schemes by crooked gamblers, even a pirate, and has learned how to protect itself. It also goes further and works just as hard to protect its clients from larceny-minded visitors.

Many tourists coming to the casino for the first time, particularly Americans, are completely unfamiliar with gambling and are the targets of confidence men. One such woman, from Wichita, Kansas, was approached by a man who whispered that he had a tip for her. He led her to a corner and explained that he and the croupier at table No. 2 were working together. They had a secret code: every time the croupier dropped cigar ashes on the floor, the ball on the next round would drop into red. In return for this information, the woman was to place a bet for him and the croupier. He would collect the winnings from her after each such spin.

The woman happily agreed, and a short time later she noticed that the croupier's ashes fell to the floor. With an encouraging nod from her tipster, she promptly bet on red, and just as promptly, red came up, and the man was at her elbow to collect his double share. Luck was with her three times in a row: three times she saw the ashes drop and three times red came up on the next spin, and she paid off the man each time. But something went wrong with the system. Although the croupier, a chain smoker, continued to drop ashes, black now was coming up much more frequently than red and she lost heavily. Her informant had disappeared. The angry woman sought out the manager and told her story. An immediate investigation was begun, and the croupier was exonerated. He did not know that his habit of flicking ashes to the floor had been noted by the swindler, who had used it to invent the story about its being a signal. The confidence man had a fifty-fifty chance of winning on each spin, as he did three times in a row with the woman, since red and black are equally distributed on the wheel. If he could manage to acquire a second sucker at the same table, steering one to bet on red and the other on black, he was positive of winning at least one bet before disappearing. The casino promptly put an end to this scheme by forbidding croupiers to smoke while working at the tables.

One of the cleverest schemes the casino ever ran up against was at the baccarat table. Baccarat is a card game at which the banker plays against only one player at a time, but any or all the others at the table can bet on that one player's hand against the bank by calling out "Banco." The croupier thought he had heard one of the seated men make the call, but when the play was over the man refused to pay, denying that he had shouted the word. He was a well-known industrialist, and not the kind of person who would try to get out of a losing bet. When no one else spoke up as having called banco, the puzzled croupier decided that he must have heard the shout from another table. Later that evening, the same thing happened again, this time to another patron, who also denied having made the call.

Certain now that something was brewing, the alert croupier discussed the matter with the directors. He felt sure that he would recognize the voice if he heard it again. He was instructed that if he did he was to pretend that the bank had lost, even if it held the winning hand, in order to find out who would claim having made the bet. Four days later he thought he heard the voice, and carried out his instructions. To his surprise, the man who announced himself as having placed the bet was seated in a different direction from where the voice seemingly had come. The winner was John Clark, an Englishman, whose admission to the *salons privés* had been sponsored by a prominent London society woman.

She was questioned discreetly as to Clark's background. She said that until recently she had not seen him for twelve years. "He was the rage of London society then," she recalled, "because he had a special gift for amusing guests. He is an amateur ventriloquist."

It was a wonderful system for Clark: he would throw his voice as if the bet had been made by another player at the opposite end of the table. The innocent victim, naturally enough, denied having made the bet when the bank won and the croupier wanted to collect. But if the bank lost, Clark would claim the bet. He was using this no-risk system to finance his Monte Carlo vacation, which ended abruptly that night.

During its early years, the casino hired croupiers on a seasonal basis. François Blanc could see no reason why he should pay men when the casino was closed during the summer, but he quickly changed this policy after three Turks almost got away with a quarter of a million francs, a considerable fortune at that time.

The men were seated at a *trente et quarante* table, and one of them asked for change of a 1,000-franc bill. When the money was brought to him, he unobtrusively dropped a gold coin to the floor, counted his change and complained in a loud voice that twenty francs were missing. While two attendants crept under the table to look for the coin, another player asked for a glass of water, which he clumsily spilled on a woman seated next to him. The third man got into an argument with the *chef de parti* as to whether the woman had jostled his friend's arm, causing the mishap.

This minor tempest was part of a deliberate scheme to distract attention from the croupier, who had been bribed by the trio to replace the cards in the distributing shoe with seven packs of cards stacked so that the Turks would win seven times in succession.

The coup went as planned, and the men won the fortune, but the croupier had not been able to remove all the old cards from the shoe, and the seasoned *chef de parti*, who counted to himself each card played, noticed that the croupier did not have to reshuffle after twenty-six rounds of play. He promptly stopped the game, counted the cards and found that the shoe contained more than the regulation number. The croupier confessed, and the Turks were allowed to leave after returning the money. It was after this episode that the casino instituted its policy of making a thorough investigation of all employees and keeping them on the payroll for the entire year.

This policy paid off several years later when a young croupier successfully resisted the blandishments of a beautiful Egyptian girl, who even went to the trouble of seducing him. The girl stayed away from the casino, and in the way of women, made it simple for the bachelor to meet her. She soon indicated that she had fallen in love with him, and invited him to her villa. After several such visits, she turned his thoughts to marriage and succeeded in getting him to propose. She promptly accepted, but requested a favor first.

When he said he would be happy to oblige, the girl handed him a small magnet, explained how it could be attached to the roulette table to force certain numbers to come up, and even suggested that he place the device under several tables so that they could win a great deal of money. It was obvious to the croupier that the mechanics of the plan were not those likely to be thought up by a young girl, and the suggestion that the magnets be used simultaneously on several roulette tables also indicated that a gang was involved. He realized that his easy conquest had been part of a scheme.

The croupier pretended that he would go along with her, but hurried back to the casino and reported to his superiors. The next day, the confident girl appeared at the casino with three accomplices. The officials now knew who were involved; the four were escorted to the station and placed on the first train leaving Monaco. The croupier was rewarded with a gift of 5,000 francs, and also had his memories.

Everybody in the employ of the casino management, whether he works in the hotels or in the casino itself, is trained to report any actions that are unusual.

Two middle-aged English spinster sisters, Helen and Mabel Tehern, made a splash when they arrived in Monte Carlo from South Africa. They brought with them a half million francs in cash, wanted the best and got it. Because they felt it was not proper for two ladies to go to the casino without an escort to play for them at the roulette table, they hired Harry Drummond, a former British army captain. During the first two days, Drummond won 25,000 francs for them, but his luck soon turned sour and he quickly lost that plus an additional 10,000 francs.

That night while the two sisters were dining at the Hôtel de Paris, where they were staying, their waiter heard them giggling over their losses. This was unusual enough to be reported, and Inspector Williams, of the casino, began a quiet check on them. He could not find their names listed in any publications dealing with English society. One of his aides had seen them the previous year aboard a liner operating between Southampton and Cape Town, and said that the other passengers had been shocked by their vulgar behavior. This information did little more than prove that the two women had sufficient money to travel frequently.

He still had no concrete information about the sisters the next day when they appeared at the casino, but he warned the staff to be on the alert. Drummond's luck returned, and he won 189,000 francs above his stake. The women told him they wanted to deposit the money at the Crédit Lyonnais and left the casino.

The secret of the giggling sisters was discovered several hours later when a croupier closely examined one of the 1,000-franc bills the spinsters had given Drummond to use as a stake and discovered that it was an excellent forgery. The sisters had managed to dump 300,000 forged francs on the casino. Officers soon learned that instead of going to the bank with their winnings, the sisters had left Monte Carlo.

They were arrested three weeks later in England on a warrant sent by Cape Town police. They also had flooded that area with their counterfeit bills. The sisters said that the money had been printed by a Hamburg forger, and revealed that they did not get away with as much money as the casino had thought. They later discovered that almost half of their winnings had been paid to them in their own bogus money.

Any area that attracts many wealthy people will also draw thieves to prey on them, but such matters normally are the concern of the Monaco police and not the casino. But one gentleman burglar had the casino pick the victims for him.

He was an American, Jim Roberts, and Cary Grant later used some of his exploits in the motion picture *To Catch A Thief,* but not the actual story of how Roberts was finally caught.

Roberts was a well-dressed, soft-spoken man, who always traveled first class and stopped only at the best hotels. He tipped well and lived well, his luggage was expensive and he appeared to be just another wealthy American enjoying a fling at the casino. He came to Monte Carlo year after year, and always was welcomed.

He was a frequent visitor at the casino, and late at night wandered from table to table and from salon to salon. There was nothing suspicious in this since many gamblers change tables and rooms when luck is running against them. But Roberts' prowling was part of his operations. He was on the lookout for a big winner and one who was drinking heavily. He was particularly interested in a winner who went out on a spree afterward to celebrate. This one was his victim. He would wait until the unsteady celebrant returned to his hotel room and fell into a sound sleep. Roberts observed a set of stringent rules: He opened a door only with a passkey and never damaged the lock. He always placed a piece of chloroformed cotton on the sleeper's face to make certain the victim would not awaken. He took only the man's billfold containing his money and would touch no other valuables. When he departed, he left the room exactly as he had found it.

Many of his victims never even knew they had been robbed. When they woke up the next morning with somewhat of a hang-over and could not find their wallet, they assumed they had lost it during their celebration, since their watch and other valuables were untouched.

The end of Roberts' career was anticlimactic. He broke one of his own rules and had been drinking heavily himself, and so he made a mistake when he opened a door with his master key. Instead of entering the room of his intended victim, he blundered into the room of a house detective.

The casino's own force had to go into action when its good

name was threatened by a gang of thieves who became known as "the Midnight Syndicate." This gang, organized by the Nice underworld, worked the trains that left Monte Carlo at midnight for Nice. They had men stationed at the casino to finger the winners who boarded the train. A pretty girl then would strike up an acquaintance with the man on the train, invite him to her home for a late snack and then lead him through dark and deserted streets, where he would be accosted and robbed. These attacks became so numerous—and it always was the winners who were robbed—that rumors spread that the casino was behind the plan to hijack back its losses. When Nice police were unable to stop the assaults, members of the secret casino force began to ride the trains, posing as winners. After they had made several arrests, including the women decoys, the attacks ceased.

Baroness Grone, a relative by marriage of the German imperial family, proved to be an excellent detective on her own. She had a run of luck at the roulette table and broke the bank. Since play was stopped at that time and the black crepe ceremony used, the baroness stuffed her winnings into a large handbag, which was covered with ostrich feathers, and decided to have dinner at the Hôtel de Paris. She used the underground tunnel connecting the hotel with the casino. At that time, the passage was covered with red carpet and flanked by two rows of large potted palms. While she was walking through, a hand suddenly shot out from behind one of the palms and snatched the ostrich bag. The baroness was knocked unconscious. Another guest found her a few minutes later, and when she revived she was unable to offer any description of her attacker. Resigned to her loss, and still hungry, she went to the dining room and ordered a meal. While glancing about the room, she noticed a young couple seated only two tables away from her. An ostrich feather was clinging to the trousers of the man's suit. She scribbled a note to her waiter, and three inspectors of the casino security police soon escorted the couple out of the room. They found the ostrich bag hidden under the man's belt, and the girl had secreted the stolen money under her clothes. Baroness Grone was happy to get her money back. The casino was even happier the next night, when she lost it all back at the tables. The potted palms were removed from the passage.

A sharp eye for incongruous detail led Inspector William LeQueue, of the casino security force, far afield and resulted in clearing up a murder that had baffled French police.

One of the visitors to the casino had registered as Émile Tessier, a farmer, from Bayonne. He easily stood out because he wore a black glove on his left hand which he never removed. He was a tall, hawk-nosed man, with yellowish eyes and an odd, rasping cough. When the man changed money at the cashier's desk, LeQueue noticed a third-class train ticket in his billfold. The ticket seemed out of place for a man with a well-filled wallet, who was betting 3,000 francs at a time, and the detective decided to keep his eye on him.

The man lost steadily, and finally left the casino about 11 P.M., walking through the dimly lit gardens in the direction of the railroad station. LeQueue started after him, and then lost sight of his quarry. He was about to turn back when he saw an elderly hunchback, using a cane, slowly descend the steps to the station. His first impulse was to help the man, but then the other started coughing. The detective recognized it as the cough of the tall man he had been following.

Definitely curious now, he boarded the same train and followed the man to Nice. At the station there, the hunchback darted into the shadows, and when he emerged he once again was a tall man, who walked briskly out of the station and took a cab to the Hôtel des Anglais.

LeQueue contacted police and learned that Paris detectives were seeking a hunchback wanted for the robbery murder of a moneylender. LeQueue directed them to the man he had followed, and he was the wanted man. His correct name was Bourdet, and he was known in the underworld as "the Dead Hand." His left hand had been destroyed by sulphuric acid which he had spilled during a Paris bank robbery. He had built up his hunchback disguise, lured the moneylender to his flat, murdered him and made his getaway as his normal self. He probably had noticed LeQueue following him and resorted to his hunchback disguise to cover his tracks, but his cough had given him away. Just eight weeks after LeQueue became curious about the third-class ticket, the killer was executed.

LeQueue was involved in one of the most fantastic episodes in the history of Monte Carlo, one that is still difficult to believe, and yet the record is there in LeQueue's own words. It concerned a pirate before the turn of the century, when disguised corsairs did roam the Mediterranean.

One of the steady customers at the casino in those days was a tall, deeply tanned man who frequently took to the seas in his beautiful pleasure yacht, *Garbino,* which originally had been constructed for the Sultan of Morocco. He always dropped anchor at Villefranche near the Christmas holidays. Although he appeared to be German, he used the name Archibald Grant.

He spoke of a large shipping line he owned, and had ready access to the best social circles. He was a heavy plunger at the casino, but a lucky one, usually winning. He finally ran into a losing streak and dropped 200,000 francs in one day. Not long afterward, Grant appeared at the manager's office and requested the return of his money. He was politely informed that the basic principle of all principles of the casino was never to return losses. Before leaving, Grant curtly informed the manager that he was in reality a privateer, that his yacht was equipped with cannons, and that if he did not receive the money aboard his yacht in two hours he would blast the casino to rubble.

Camille Blanc, the head of the casino, was in Paris, and the jittery manager hastily summoned the other directors. Ten minutes before the deadline a small cutter approached the *Garbino*. On board were three casino officials in top hats and morning coats. They had orders to call Grant's bluff, but prudently had brought the funds along and left them on the cutter. When they boarded the yacht, they discovered that Grant had not been joking, that he had four cannons aboard and that they were primed and pointing at the casino. The basic principle of the casino went overboard as the money hurriedly changed hands.

The embarrassed casino officials kept quiet and hushed up the affair, but at least had the satisfaction of barring Grant from the gaming rooms. The pirate resented this and plotted to get revenge. He waited for two years, and then struck.

The casino had hired a new young detective, LeQueue, who knew nothing about the previous incident. On his first day off, he was sitting at the bar in the Hôtel Hermitage when a man whom he described later as about fifty, with a leathery face, a gray goatee and gleaming blue eyes, started talking to him. The man was Grant, and he knew that LeQueue was employed by the casino. They chatted about the place. Grant spoke familiarly about the *salons privés,* and since the detective knew that regular patrons there were carefully screened he was not suspicious when Grant invited him to dinner aboard his yacht. Here are LeQueue's own words on what followed:

"Grant took me to the *Garbino,* which lay completely in the dark. Only a small blue night lamp was burning on top of the mainmast. I saw no sign of life aboard, except for a fleeting shadow who received us.

"We entered a brightly lit salon that was filled with thick

carpets, wall mirrors and heavy black silk curtains. The table was covered with expensive crystal and silver, and there were bottles of champagne in a bucket.

"After dinner, a Negro in red livery came in and Grant whispered something into his ear. The servant grinned, left the room and came back with a box of cigars that seemed a little strong to me. As I smoked, I suddenly began to feel ill. My host's features dissolved before my eyes, the outlines of the room became blurred and my tongue got so heavy that I could no longer utter a word."

When LeQueue woke up in a narrow cabin, it was daylight and the yacht was out on the open sea. He hurried to the bridge, where a plump, mustached captain was scanning the horizon with a telescope. LeQueue asked for Grant and was told that the other had left the ship. When he demanded to be returned to shore, a sailor with a knife in his belt told him to return to his cabin. The crew of thirty men seemed to have been hand-picked from the scum of Mediterranean ports.

The following morning the yacht anchored in a small, isolated bay off the coast of North Africa, and the crew went to work converting the vessel into a warship. Cannons were brought up from the hold; the name of the ship was blacked out and replaced with the name *Cagne*. Dummy fittings were installed to give the yacht the appearance of a French cannon boat. For two days the vessel lay in wait; and from conversation LeQueue overheard, they were waiting for the British freighter *Macclesfield,* en route from Liverpool to Constantinople with a shipment of gold. When the freighter finally came into view, the disguised yacht, flying the French flag, fired a warning shot, signaling the other vessel to stop. The freighter captain pointed to the Union Jack he was flying, shouted that it must be a mistake and continued on his way. The disguised vessel promptly opened fire and scored a hit on one of the freighter's funnels. The pirates boarded the ship, told the stunned captain that France and England were at war, removed the gold and fled.

LeQueue was equally stunned at what he witnessed, and told the captain that he would be hanged for piracy. The other man shouted with laughter, pointed to the detective and told him that he was the one who would be hanged. He showed LeQueue a bill of sale, signed by Grant, in which the detective was listed as the new owner of the vessel. The crew had orders that if they were captured they were to blame LeQueue and the Monte Carlo Casino for the piracy act. The disguised vessel put in at another bay, was quickly reconverted into the pleasure yacht and made its way back to southern France. LeQueue was put ashore and warned to keep his mouth shut. To his relief, the bill of sale was destroyed.

The attack on the freighter caused a sensation in England, and the British ambassador in Paris presented a bill for damages. Although the French Government denied any knowledge or responsibility, it paid the bill.

LeQueue hurried back to Monte Carlo with his incredible story, not daring to expect that he would be believed and expecting to be fired. But casino officials, who had had one experience with Grant, did not doubt his story at all, and he rose in time to head their detective force.

Some years later a German liner reported that a yacht had attempted to attack it off the Italian island of Gorgona. The liner rammed the vessel and sank it, and said it could find no survivors. From a description, LeQueue was certain that it had been the *Garbino,* and he finally told outsiders his story of the pirate who had threatened to destroy Monte Carlo.

CHAPTER 11

A Churchill Tragedy

If a former President of the United States were to fall from bed and break a hip in a hotel owned by a Las Vegas gambling casino, the shock that would sweep the country at his presence there might be recorded on a seismograph. But when this did happen to Sir Winston Churchill at Monte Carlo, no eyebrows were raised in England or elsewhere.

The man who many historians believe has been the greatest Prime Minister in England's greatest hour of need has never concealed his delight in the joys of a big, fat cigar, a good glass of brandy or the gaming tables of the Monte Carlo Casino. During World War II when a British submarine, in a brilliant feat of marksmanship, angled a torpedo through an 18-foot-wide entrance into Monte Carlo's port and sank a mine sweeper, Churchill sent the commander a cable of congratulations and wound up with the quip, "And now please don't go to the casino and lose your money there." And it was a run of luck at the roulette wheel at the Monte Carlo Casino that may have influenced Sir Winston not to oppose the marriage of his daughter Sarah to Antony Beauchamp. This was the belief of Beauchamp, expressed personally to one of us.

Beauchamp was a handsome, slim, dark-haired man with vivid blue eyes. During the war he served under General Wingate in Burma and later saw service in Italy. A gifted photographer, he came into his own after the war, when he specialized in women's portraits. Although he was a society photographer, he was not himself of society, but was the son of a London art teacher named Entwistle, and had grown up in typical English middle-class surroundings. He adopted the name Beauchamp for business reasons. Although he had known Sarah Churchill for some years, it was only on a professional basis, having taken her picture at various functions.

Their casual acquaintance quickened in the spring of 1948 when they met by chance in the lobby of a London hotel and chatted. They found they liked each other, and they began to go out on dates. Within a short time they were in love, and Sarah finally invited Tony to the Churchill family home at Chartwell to present him to her parents, a prelude to a possible engagement and marriage.

But no engagement announcement followed the visit. Sir Winston had reason to caution against haste, having witnessed one unfortunate marriage for this daughter. While appearing as an actress in a London musical show, Sarah had fallen in love with its leading comedian, Vic Oliver, a man sixteen years her senior. Oliver, whose real name was Viktor Samek, had come to the United States from Vienna after World War I and established himself as a successful entertainer. When the musical closed in London, he returned to the United States, and Sarah, not long afterward, also went there. The Churchills sent her brother Randolph after her in an attempt to prevent the marriage, but the couple were wed on Christmas Eve, 1936, at City Hall, in New York City.

During the next three years, Sarah traveled about the

United States with Oliver as he performed in various night clubs, but she was a Churchill, and when World War II broke out she hurried home to England, where she volunteered as a Wren. As part of her official duties she accompanied her father to the history-making conferences at Teheran, Cairo and Yalta.

Her wartime experiences changed her outlook, and when peace came she no longer was content to resume the nomadic type of life she had been leading. She and Oliver became estranged, and were divorced in 1945.

Although Beauchamp could understand Sir Winston's reluctance to approve the marriage without some further thought, he knew that he had not caught Sarah on any rebound; three years had passed since her divorce. He realized that he was not a product of England's fashionable misnamed public schools, but he also knew that the Churchills were well known for their lack of snobbishness. But it also was true that there were titled peers of the realm as well as men who had attained knighthood for their achievements who were more than momentarily interested in the vivacious and lovely-looking Sarah.

Beauchamp was delighted when he received an invitation during the summer of 1948 to come to Monte Carlo for a week as the guest of the Churchills. As he said wryly later, he knew he was going to be scrutinized thoroughly, and hoped that he would make a favorable impression.

On his first night there, he was invited to have dinner with the Churchills at the Hôtel de Paris. As he entered the dining room at the appointed hour, he found the Churchill party already seated. Sir Winston stood up and waved to him, while other diners craned their necks to see whom the distinguished statesman was greeting. Tony hurried to the table, and with an expansive gesture Mr. Churchill said to the others there, "May I introduce Mr. Beauchamp, one of

England's best photographers." In addition to Mrs. Churchill and Sarah, those present included a Churchill relative from the United States and the Duke and Duchess of Westminster.

In the days that followed, Tony Beauchamp found himself moving in a select circle. He was invited along with the Churchills to a different dinner party almost every night. One evening it was at the villa of the Duke and Duchess of Windsor, then living on the Cap d'Antibes. Tony later said of this visit:

"When we reached the villa, I was impressed by the regal splendor in which the duke and duchess continued to live. The duke clearly maintained habits of a lifetime, and we were received by our host and hostess in an exceedingly elegant drawing room. It was all white—white carpets, white furniture, white flowers."

Sarah's dinner partner that evening was former King Michael of Rumania, while Beauchamp was seated next to his wife, Princess Anne. With Sir Winston present, it was quite natural that many of the discussions should revolve around politics, but though Tony could discourse on many subjects he had no interest in politics and could contribute little to the conversation, a not too happy situation for a young man hoping to become Winston Churchill's son-in-law.

He and Sarah spent the daylight hours exploring the hilly streets and byways, strolling hand in hand, but whenever Tony and Sir Winston were together neither brought up what was uppermost in their minds, the question of Tony's marriage to Sarah. Toward the close of the week, Beauchamp felt that the elderly statesman was looking even more grim in his presence. He discovered that Churchill would thaw each time he listened to Charles Trenet's "La Mer," a popular tune of the moment, and so he arranged to have the band play the song every time they dined at the hotel.

At lunch one day, knowing of Churchill's interest in roulette, he mentioned that Prince Leon Radziwill, a distant relative of the Prince Leon Radziwill once connected with the casino, had told him about a system he had been using. Tony added that he intended to try it before he left.

Sir Winston glanced at him and remarked that if he planned to gamble he hoped Beauchamp had the foresight to have first purchased his return ticket to England. He then asked how the prince had made out with his system.

Beauchamp smiled. "It helped him lose his money a little more slowly."

This was a jest with bitter truth in it. Many different branches of the Radziwills, one of Poland's oldest noble families, had escaped during the Nazi invasion, abandoning vast holdings and treasures. The Leon Radziwills had managed to take along some of the jewels and had taken refuge in Monte Carlo. By selling off their gems one at a time, they had managed to live through the war years in some comfort at the Hôtel Continental. When his wife died in 1946, Prince Radziwill sought solace at the gaming tables and was virtually penniless when Beauchamp spoke to him. After the prince had explained his system, the photographer asked why he was not playing it and making money. The prince shrugged and replied that that was the trouble, he had played it too often. "It works only the first time," he added. He died later in poverty in Paris.

Beauchamp's remarks about roulette bore fruit two days later, during the final hours of his week's visit. He dined that last night in the hotel with the Churchills, and during dinner Sir Winston turned to him and said, "I think I am going to try my luck tonight. Antony, we will go to the casino together."

Only two hours remained. Beauchamp was leaving on the eleven-thirty train. The two men walked through the tunnel leading directly from the Hôtel de Paris into the gaming rooms. Churchill, as always, was accompanied by Detective Thompson, his bodyguard. Tony decided to test Prince Radziwill's system. Here, in his own words, is what happened:

"I won and won. Churchill watched me closely. After a while he instructed me to put down his chips in the same manner. I did, and our luck held. The chips piled up higher and higher in front of us. Sir Winston beamed. He puffed appreciatively at his cigar. He began to take a more benevolent view of roulette systems in general and of myself in particular."

By 11 P.M. it was time for the guest to bid farewell to his host. They cashed in their chips, and Beauchamp hurried off to make his train. They still had exchanged no words about Tony's wish to marry Sarah. When Sir Winston returned to the hotel, he saw his daughter. He was puffing on his inevitable cigar and was carrying a bundle of bank notes. As Sarah later told Tony, her father said to her, "Rather a clever young man, your Antony."

There was no need for further conversation. Sarah now knew her father would not oppose the engagement. Perhaps Beauchamp was correct in thinking the spinning roulette wheel had assisted him in the romance, and he had won the one game he really wanted.

The elated couple soon were busy making plans for the future. Sarah's hopes for a successful acting career still had not been realized. For the past few years she had been on tour in the small towns of England with the thriller *Gaslight,* and had played minor roles in two Italian movies, but she now was thirty-four years old and no London producers were beating paths to her door with offers of starring or important roles in forthcoming productions. Her theatrical career seemed at a dead end.

Beauchamp had faith in her ability, and he suggested that she go to the United States and renew her career there.

He also had plans for himself. Although recognized as one of the best photographers in England, he was not content to remain a photographer. He wanted to broaden his horizon and become an author, a director and a producer of television and motion picture films. He also wanted to go to the United States and launch his new career there. The two of them discussed their future; perhaps Sarah would star in films he produced.

As part of their strategy to make the United States aware of Sarah Churchill, Antony Beauchamp began taking hundreds of photographs of her. He knew ordinary portraits failed to capture the true beauty and charm of her green eyes, auburn hair and classic profile. Fleeting expressions appeared and vanished in the constant movement of her mobile features. He purchased new equipment, including a camera that could take color pictures at the speed of one forty thousandth of a second, to capture her radiance.

When Beauchamp was finally satisfied with the pictures he took, Miss Churchill flew to New York to stay as a house guest with her father's old friend, Bernard Baruch. And Tony submitted his photographs to *Life* magazine. Ten days later, on May 23, 1949, millions of Americans began to appreciate the true beauty of Miss Churchill when they saw her color photograph on the cover of *Life*.

The first part of the plan had been successful. The tremendous publicity she had received and her good looks impressed American theatrical producers, and she received many offers. The following month she went on tour, starring in *The Philadelphia Story* and playing the same role that was to be acted later by Grace Kelly in the movie *High Society*, Miss Kelly's last production before she became Princess of Monaco.

The tour was a personal triumph for Miss Churchill, and critics praised her acting ability wherever she appeared.

When the tour was over, she and Tony put into action the second part of their plan. On October 17, 1949, Sarah Churchill and Antony Beauchamp were married at Sea Island, Georgia. A reporter who was present at the ceremony wrote:

"The two were slightly tipsy—before the ceremony, during the ceremony, and after the ceremony—they were visibly drunk with happiness. I do not believe they understood a word of what was being said. But no one could doubt the seriousness of their intentions."

It was inevitable now that Sarah would receive her chance in the movies, and she was signed by Metro-Goldwyn-Mayer to appear as the partner of Fred Astaire in the musical comedy *Royal Wedding*. The Beauchamps took a house in Beverly Hills, and it soon became a favorite meeting place for many stars.

Tony Beauchamp was accepted into the Churchill family. When Sir Winston visited President Truman in 1951, Sarah and Tony were invited to the White House. The following year when Anthony Eden married Sir Winston's niece Clarissa, Beauchamp was asked to take all the official wedding pictures.

But the spinning wheel of fortune that had been so right for Tony Beauchamp that night in Monte Carlo now spun off in another direction. Sarah's career was safely under way, and she appeared in starring roles on many television shows, but Tony was unable to break out of his classification as a photographer. He was in demand, he could get all the work he wanted and command high fees, but as a photographer. No studio wanted to gamble on his belief that he would make an excellent director or producer.

With the doors still closed to him in the United States in that direction, he returned to London in 1953 and established a television agency. His first venture was a series of thirteen half-hour films based on the career of detective Fabian of

Scotland Yard. Beauchamp had hoped that Sarah would play the feminine lead in the series, but she had so many contractual obligations in the United States that she was unable to leave. The series made money for Tony's backers, but not a great deal for him.

Newspaper columnists hinted that the couple had drifted apart. One of Beauchamp's partners was quoted as saying, "Antony is embittered. He feels that he has contributed his share to Sarah's fame in the United States. He does not expect any gratitude—that would be silly. But after all, every man has his pride."

On the other side of the coin, one of Sarah's friends was quoted as saying, "Mr. Beauchamp is a complicated man. He does not know the value of money. He is as much attracted by other women as they feel attracted by him."

The two principals maintained their own silence.

In January, 1956, a triumphant Miss Churchill returned to London to star in a TV documentary about the city. She went at once to the apartment she and Tony maintained in Ebury Street, where he had his studio. The place was empty. Beauchamp had left a few hours earlier. There were no plans to use his services in making his wife's film.

Beauchamp appeared in Monte Carlo, where he was seen wandering the same streets he and Sarah had walked eight years earlier. One night he went to the casino and played the same system he had used with Winston Churchill. Prince Radziwill had been wrong in stating it worked only the first time. Once again the chips piled up in front of him, but either he lost interest or it evoked too many memories. He suddenly stopped playing, cashed the chips and went to Italy.

Upon his return to London, after Sarah had gone back to the United States, Beauchamp almost completely abandoned his once-thriving photography studio as he plunged ahead in his desire to achieve a new career. He discussed plans to shoot a Cinemascope movie about the British spy heroine Christina Granville. He bought the rights for a TV series entitled "Six Girls and a Man." He also was busy planning a London stage version of *Gigi*. None of these projects got off the ground.

Meanwhile, his debts mounted. None of his friends nor Sarah knew of his financial plight; he was too proud to ask for any help, though he did tell friends that he felt British society had not forgiven him for the manner in which he had crashed it. In August, 1957, a London newspaper wrote the end of the story for him when it headlined:

ANTONY BEAUCHAMP FOUND DEAD IN HIS FLAT. CHURCHILL'S SON-IN-LAW COMMITS SUICIDE IN A FIT OF DEPRESSION

The report of her husband's self-destruction was a shattering blow to Miss Churchill. "I should have rejoined him on the Riviera," she tearfully told friends, and recalled that her father's favorite nickname for her was "the Mule." She could not be consoled, and several months later was arrested on a charge of public intoxication, collapsed and had to be hospitalized. As soon as she was able to travel, she flew to join her father, who was staying at a villa near Monte Carlo. And she now was seen visiting all the places where she and Tony Beauchamp once had strolled.

Hoping to distract her, Aristotle Onassis, the owner of the casino, invited Sarah and her father for a cruise along the Italian coast. Not long after the yacht had put out to sea, it made a quick return. Sir Winston had been shaken by his daughter's plight more deeply than he realized, and became critically ill. The statesman, then eighty-three, was rushed to a hospital, and his wife and other children were summoned from London to his bedside. He remained in acute danger for a week, then passed the crisis and recovered. The shock of her father's serious illness also helped Sarah overcome her own crisis, and she returned once more to her career.

And at the casino each night the croupiers can be heard chanting their long-familiar call which pretends that no ladies are present, although women frequently outnumber the men at a table:

"Messieurs, faites vos jeux! Les jeux sont faits? Rien ne va plus!"

It is only in the make-believe world of the casino that every few moments you are offered a last chance and a new opportunity to change fate.

CHAPTER 12

Plungers and Players

On August 2, 1962, a Thursday, Khalil Bedas, a visitor from Lebanon, arrived in Monte Carlo accompanied by his secretary and three companions. They entered one of the salons, where the visitor sat down at a roulette table and played steadily for many hours. His companions were busy; one kept him supplied with his favorite beverage, another saw to it that a cigarette was always ready, and the third kept careful watch over his chips. When he left the casino, hc had won some $200,000. He then flew to Baden-Baden, where it is reported that he won an additional $50,000, and on his third day he was in Deauville, where word soon spread that he had dropped all his winnings and lost a good sum of his own money. On Monday morning he was back at his desk in Beirut.

Sound like fiction? An invention by E. Phillips Oppenheim? It is neither; it is fact.

Mr. Bedas, one of the wealthiest men in the Arab world—some say only King Saud is richer—is the owner of a large hotel chain, three airlines and as many banks. He is of that small group of men known in the casino world as plungers—

the big bettors. He can afford to gamble, often wins or loses large sums, and has flown to Las Vegas to spend a weekend there. He looks upon gambling as a distraction, a way of easing the tensions that accompany his work as a busy and successful businessman. He is a frequent visitor to Monte Carlo, and croupiers there rated him as the biggest gambler of the 1962 season.

Jack L. Warner, the Hollywood producer, is a legendary figure among plungers, and since he is considered one of the finest baccarat players these games to him are tests of will power and self-control. He once won $300,000 from ex-King Farouk of Egypt in two weeks. His favorite gambling partners have included his movie colleagues Darryl Zanuck and Sam Spiegel, as well as ex-Emperor Bao Dai; the Shah of Iran; Jaime Silberain, Spanish industrialist; Robert Barnet, New York diamond merchant; Pedro Haroin, Brazilian coffee magnate; Alexander Nicoloudis, Greek ship line owner; and composer Frederick Loewe, who hit his own golden jackpot with *My Fair Lady*.

Warner's table at the Monte Carlo Casino is always surrounded by sightseers since the stakes are usually high. He lost $150,000 one night within a few hours, and then invited the winners to drink champagne. He won back part of his losses the next day. After winning $60,000 another night, he placed the money in his safe in his villa on Cap d'Antibes and went to Rome on business. Thieves who had heard about his winnings guessed correctly where the money would be and looted the safe.

Like most of the plungers, he is a restless player, and will switch from casino to casino. He has left the Monte Carlo Casino late at night, and then spent the hours to dawn at the Palm Beach Casino, in Cannes. His greatest coup came on August 13, 1957, when he, Zanuck, Haroin and several other friends, playing baccarat, bucked and literally broke the bank at the Palm Beach Casino. He won 40 million francs; Zanuck, Haroin and several others, 20 million each. The casino lost 340 million francs that night, almost one million dollars.

But the victory was short-lived. The night was still young, Warner wanted to go on playing and he and Haroin came to Monte Carlo, where their winnings melted away.

On his sixty-sixth birthday, in August, 1958, a group of friends gave Warner a surprise party. Four nights later he staged his own celebration by winning $50,000, but was critically injured in an automobile accident on his way home. He was in a coma for four days, but finally recovered, and just one year later won $120,000 from Prince Talal of Saudi Arabia.

Edward Gilbert, the young business executive who fled to Brazil when a stock market crash wiped out his personal empire, and then later voluntarily returned to face the charges against him, was one of the high plungers at Monte Carlo for several years. He gambled so heavily that the casino waived one of its rules and allowed him to enter the private rooms in sports clothes.

Gambling for high stakes can be an insidious disease unless one has the will power to stop at the right time, or sufficient money not to mind the losses. Darry Cowl, a young and very popular French comedian, almost wrecked his career in 1960 and disappeared from the screen for almost two years because of the gambling bug. He has given a graphic description of what can happen:

"Financial success had come too quickly for me, and I acquired a terrible vice: gambling. I had always been a gambler, but at the beginning of my career I only played poker games where I might lose twenty or thirty dollars.

"Then suddenly I became a star. Within two years I had made thirty films. As soon as I appeared on the screen, the audience would start roaring before I even opened my mouth. I thought this would go on forever.

"I practically installed myself in Monte Carlo. I stayed in the casino from opening to closing time. When I had signed up for a movie, I took the next plane to Monte Carlo and gambled away my whole fee in one night. In the past two years I spent all my weekends in Monte Carlo. I was really sick. I lost over four hundred thousand dollars that way.

"One day, after having lost fifty thousand, I called my impresario in Paris and told him I was ready to sign any contract for any role, even if I didn't know a single word of the scenario, provided he sent me more money. I soon accepted more roles than I could possibly work into my schedule. I was like drugged. When the casino closed, I would often go on playing poker with the waiters in the last bar that was still open. One night I won seventy thousand. The next morning, I went into all the shops and bought things for three thousand dollars. That same evening, I lost the remaining money and sold what I had just bought for a total of five hundred dollars."

He finally met a girl who cured him of his gambling addiction, and straightened out his career. He signed a Hollywood contract. During the 1962 season he returned to Monte Carlo and watched people play for an hour without getting an urge to join them. He sighed happily and said he now knew he was cured.

In August of 1962, Monte Carlo's fear of suicide returned when Bella Darvi, a movie actress, took an overdose of sleeping pills after she had lost all her money in the casino. A friend broke into her room and saved her life.

The greatest gambler in Monte Carlo's history was Nicholas Zogrophos, who was the front man for a Greek snydicate. He did not gamble for pleasure; it was a science, a business and an art to him. He took part in the largest single recorded money game of baccarat, in which he was banker, and the Aga Khan, the French Automobile maker Citroen and James Hennessy, the liquor and brandy manufacturer, united against him. He lost 1.2 million dollars that night.

Like those of many of his countrymen who acquire great wealth, his past is obscured by legend. It is said that he started his career as a shepherd in the hills of Illyria and later became a clerk in a London luxury hotel, where he made the acquaintance of Athanasios Vagliano, a ship owner. The latter, impressed by his mathematical wizardry, hired him, and both men became very wealthy during World War I, transporting goods for Basil Zaharoff under a neutral flag.

During the 1920's, Zogrophos and Vagliano founded a Greek syndicate that challenged the baccarat players of Europe. Zogrophos represented the group at Monte Carlo. Since the casino was not banking the games, but receiving a cut on the play, the only limit was up to the banker, and Zogrophos met any challenge. Sacha Guitry called him a walking calculating machine. The Greek player denied that baccarat was a game of luck; he said it was a game of skill that required as much attention as a champion chess player gave to his moves.

"Everything is a matter of mathematics," he explained. "There are only three kinds of cards: strong, weak or mediocre. One must be able to figure out within seconds what they are worth and whether it is smart to draw a third card."

For nineteen years Zogrophos played against some of the richest men in the world. He never lost his nerve, took every bet and never showed the slightest sign of emotion. "When I win it would be tactless to show that I am content," he said, "and when I lose it would be unwise to betray my dismay."

He said that a great gambler must have a good stomach and a sturdy heart. If he did not, his stomach might betray him and his face would turn pale, or his heart would give him away and he would get red in the face. He claimed he could read the faces of most of the men he played against. When he learned that he had an ulcer, he stopped playing for a year, until his ailment was cured.

At one point, he lost for eight successive days, and he hit upon a psychological trick to reduce the amount of the bets against him while he was on this losing streak. He had the casino remove the 50,000-franc plaques that were normally used at his table and had them replaced with 10,000-franc chips. He reasoned that his opponents would hesitate to push out a big pile of chips when they were accustomed to using just one or two.

Many gamblers try to retrieve their losses by doubling up on their bets, and Zogrophos considered such men poor players. He neither smoked nor drank alcohol, but constantly sipped mineral water, and his diet consisted of fruits, vegetables and grilled meat. He drank wine at the tables just once, when a Frenchman opposing him won 12 million francs in the first fifteen minutes of play. He called for a glass of cold champagne, sipped it slowly and then won the money back.

He finally retired from active gambling in 1939 and bought the Palm Beach Casino, in Cannes, with the money he had won at Monte Carlo.

One of the big plungers at Monte Carlo at that time was fashion designer Jean Patou, who also surrounded himself with beautiful women, fast cars and speedboats. When friends told him that he was gambling too heavily, he claimed that it helped his publicity, that every million francs he lost brought him two million francs in business. But his gambling losses continued to mount faster than his business, and he died in poverty.

The chief cashier of a Belgian coal mine, who had stolen one million francs, was one of the luckiest gamblers at Monte Carlo. He had sent the management a post card from Brussels in which he said that he had become ill from fish poisoning and would be back in three or four days. The suspicious directors checked and discovered the money missing. The company was thrown off because the post card had been mailed from Brussels, and did not know where to look for him.

The cashier began to play for high stakes at the casino, but he had made the mistake of renting a room in a private home, which he usually did on his vacation. Since guests who gambled for large stakes did not normally stay at inexpensive rooming houses, Monaco police questioned the man, and he confessed.

They had no order as yet for his arrest, and could not take him into custody, but he was ordered not to leave the principality. The cashier decided to take one last chance at the casino. He returned to the gaming room and began scattering his chips with reckless abandon all over the green baize. He won three million francs in two hours.

The cashier now had the money he had stolen, and a large stake of his own as well. He hurried to the casino's writing room and wrote his firm a letter in which he said:

"You are wrong if you believe that I wanted to steal the missing funds. On the contrary, I intended to save them. Last Friday night I had a dream that a burglar would break into our cashbox the following Sunday. I didn't tell you about my vision because you would have taunted me. Instead, I took the funds with me to keep watch over them. As you don't seem to trust me any longer, I herewith hand in my resignation. The saved million will be returned to you by postal order."

The cashier did return the money, the firm withdrew its charges and the cashier later opened a successful stationery business. Camille Blanc, who was director of the casino then, and thought system players were sure to lose, drew the only moral to this incident. He said that if the cashier had played a system he probably would have lost and wound up in prison.

In a happier vein was the luck of a little servant girl who was brought to Monte Carlo as a chambermaid by two sisters, who left her flat without any money when they went off with two wealthy men. The girl had a little dog, and she trained him to go begging from table to table in restaurants, but to pick up only gold coins. This so amused the dinner patrons that the girl succeeded in getting together a small stake, and she risked it all on one spin of the wheel. She won and collected enough money to buy a farm in the hills back of Monte Carlo.

Noel Coward was an absent-minded gambler, and occasionally would wander off, forgetting that he left a bet on the roulette table. He did this one night, and his stake grew into a large pile of chips. A young Englishman from a good family, but down on his luck, noticed this and wanted to claim the chips, but feared that the croupier would challenge him. He approached the noted writer-entertainer, whom he knew slightly, and told him that his prospective father-in-law had just entered the casino, that he did not want him to know that he had been gambling heavily, and was afraid to pick up his winnings at table No. 5. He pointed to the pile of chips and asked Coward if he would pick it up for him. He still had a graceful way out at this moment because if Coward recognized that they were his own chips he could have laughed it off as a joke. The obliging Coward went to the table, picked up his own pile of chips and unsuspectingly handed it over to the other man. Years later, after he became a successful broker in London, this man publicly bragged about the incident.

One of the strangest roulette games that took place in the Monte Carlo Casino occurred in 1921. The object: to win an empire. And the stake involved in the actual betting was no small sum, a half million Swiss francs.

This unusual episode in history began in March of that year in Prangins, Switzerland, where ex-Emperor Karl of Austria was living in exile with his young wife, Zita. The previous year Hungary had voted for the return of the monarchy and Admiral Horthy had been appointed regent. Karl considered himself once again King of Hungary, and was impatient to be returned to his throne, but the Little Entente was against the move.

With no advance warning or notice, Karl set off secretly, and alone, for Vienna, using his gardener's passport. From there he went by car to the royal castle on the hills of Buda, where he stormed into Horthy's office. The regent ordered him to return to Switzerland, saying that conditions were too unsettled for him to reclaim the throne as yet. He became critically ill, but when he recovered he returned to Switzerland. Since he had violated the terms of his exile, the Swiss Government moved him to Hertenstein Castle, where he could be watched more closely. He had to sign a pledge that he would make no more premature attempts to regain his throne.

His ambitious wife, Zita, now took over and began writing secret messages, hoping to stir up action. Two Hungarian officers came forth with a scheme to fly Karl to Budapest and announce a *coup d'état,* but as Zita pointed out, this required money and the former king had no funds.

These two officers then enlisted the aid of a Viennese countess, and they began soliciting funds from the old noble families of Hungary who wanted the monarchy restored; they collected the 500,000 Swiss francs. But the conspirators felt they needed millions more for a thorough propaganda campaign to proceed with the march on Budapest. One of the officers was certain that he had an unbeatable system at roulette, and they hurried to Monte Carlo to win enough money to place Karl back on the throne. Like almost all roulette systems, this one also failed to work, and the money was lost. Later, when the original backers demanded an accounting of the funds, the countess told Karl what they had done. He was deeply distressed, and promised that he would pay back the money. The Hungarian nobles, after checking with Monte Carlo officials and learning that the story was true, dropped the matter. The desperate royal couple decided to go ahead anyway and make a dramatic flight, hoping that their sudden appearance would rally the people to their side. They rented a small plane which got lost, and had to make a forced landing in eastern Hungary. This alerted the government, and when their train neared Budapest it was stopped by troops and the royal pair were ignominiously bundled back to Switzerland. The Allied Control Commission ordered them moved to Madeira, and Karl died there four months later, his dream of restoring the Hapsburg Empire shattered on the roulette tables of Monte Carlo.

As mentioned earlier, former King Farouk of Egypt was a heavy plunger while he occupied the throne, and he did not allow exile to interfere with his gambling. His appetite for food was as prodigious. Other players had to wait while he emptied an entire can of caviar. He has been observed on many occasions at 6 A.M., after a night at the gaming tables, consuming six roast chickens.

The Aga Khan is the spiritual leader of a large segment of the Mohammedan sect, and since Farouk is a descendant of Mohammed Ali, the Aga occasionally paid homage to the ex-king. Not too long before his death, the elderly Aga limped into the casino restaurant, where Farouk was seated, and painfully bent his knee before him. Farouk did not arise to greet the spiritual leader, but went on eating his chicken. The Aga got to his feet and slowly withdrew, walking backward. At the exit, one of Farouk's servants handed him a cup of coffee. The Aga's wife, the Begum, was angry at the treatment he had received, but the Aga Khan shrugged and told her, *"C'est la tradition."*

Farouk is considered one of the top baccarat players in Europe, and prides himself on keeping his facial muscles under control. He was playing against an Englishman one night and lost $12,000 without displaying any sign of emotion. The man opposite him also sat motionless. Farouk hastily summoned an attendant. His opponent had died of a heart attack after winning.

The former sovereign of Egypt is not the most popular man on the Riviera with some people, and to the delight of some of his detractors, he was involved in one of the slickest confidence schemes along the resort area.

It began in 1951, while Farouk was still on the throne, with the arrival of a man who carried a passport bearing a seal certifying that it had been issued by the Spanish consulate in Milan. His name was given as Fernández Novarro. The newcomer rented an expensive hotel suite and began betting heavily at the gaming tables. Since he had put up the proper front, was amply supplied with cash and his papers seemed to be in order, he avoided any close scrutiny by Monaco police. He did not seem to mind his large losses, and vaguely mentioned tin mines in Peru.

He also entertained on a large scale and tipped like a multimillionaire on a spree, and admiring headwaiters made sure to introduce him to all the notables. One of those he met was King Farouk, whom he promptly challenged to a game of baccarat, and a friendship developed between the men.

With his beachhead firmly established on the Riviera, Novarro began mentioning that his present wealth was trifling compared to what he would have if he could get his hands on money he had hidden in safe-deposit vaults in the

United States. He indicated that he had 60 million dollars hidden there under various aliases, illegal profits he had made during Prohibition while serving as one of Al Capone's trusted aides.

"In Chicago, I was known as Kid Tiger," he confided. "My job was to arrange the shipments of booze from Canada."

He said that Federal Treasury agents were on the lookout for him, that they knew he had money hidden and wanted him for income tax evasion. He said he would be happy to pay a 10 per cent commission to anybody who could smuggle the money out for him.

King Farouk was one of those to whom he told his story. The monarch was interested, and Novarro mentioned that he would like an advance of $100,000 to keep him going because of his heavy casino losses. The king had to return to Egypt for a while, and in April, 1952, Novarro arrived at the Hotel Semiramis, in Cairo, for further discussions. He proposed that Farouk dispatch a special courier to the United States who would carry authorization to open the vaults and then could bring the money back in diplomatic pouches. In exchange for this, he offered to invest between 20 and 30 per cent of the salvaged funds in Egypt. He also proposed to boost tourist trade by using some of the money to open a gambling casino on the Nile, in which the Egyptian Government would own 51 per cent of the shares. Negotiations stalled when Farouk demanded guarantees which Novarro was unwilling to give him.

When Farouk was overthrown and went into exile on the Riviera, he learned that Novarro was a swindler and had been peddling variations of his hidden-treasure story for many years. Police records show that his actual name was Abram Sykowski and that he had been born in Poland. His family migrated to the United States when he was a boy, and he had grown up in the slums of New York City's Lower East

Side. His police record started when he was twenty, in Cuba, where he was arrested for cheating a tourist out of forty dollars.

He had been in Chicago for a while, but if he had been part of the Capone gang it must have been as a very minor cog, because he was arrested in 1923 and received a long prison sentence. Released in 1929, he became an itinerant con man, and his trail led from Hamburg to Madrid, Vienna, Zurich, Rome, Barcelona; finally to Montreal, where he arrived shortly before the outbreak of the war.

He stayed at the Mount Royal Hotel, in Montreal, and used both the Novarro alias and the hidden-treasure story for the first time. He posed as Count Alexander Novarro Fernández, a cousin of the late King Alfonso XII of Spain. When doubters jokingly proposed to stick pins into him to see whether he had hemophilia, he drew himself up and shouted, "Don't you ever touch a person of royal blood!"

The swindler was even more generous there with his first story, claiming he had 340 million cached in thirty-four different banks. A group of wealthy Canadians, including an official of an airline, advanced him $125,000 to buy a secret code book showing the locations of the banks. He left the country aboard one of his victim's own passenger planes.

He next did a tour of South American countries, and was arrested by the FBI in September, 1946, when he stepped off a plane in Miami. He served a three-year sentence, and then was deported to Cuba in 1949, appearing two years later on the Riviera, where he started "Operation Farouk."

The former king and several other prominent figures on the Riviera filed a complaint against him, and when he returned from Switzerland, in January, 1953, he was picked up at the border and assigned to a forced residence in Aurillac as an undesirable alien, required to report to the station house three times a day. He managed to escape in the winter

of 1957 and disappeared. He was not seen in Monte Carlo
again.

The unsettled conditions in some South American countries brought noted players to Monte Carlo. Before Perón
was ousted as dictator of Argentina, he seized the shipping
lines of Albert Dodero, though he did give him a token payment of 26 million pesos for the more valuable line. Dodero
had anticipated this move and managed to send abroad a
large part of his fortune, so that when he came to the Riviera
he had a daily income of $2,500.

He rented the Château des Pins, near Monte Carlo, and
seemed determined to spend as much of his fortune as he
could. He began holding simultaneous parties, and would
rush from a cocktail affair he was giving in Cannes to a ball
he was hosting in Monte Carlo. He hired a fleet of Rolls-
Royces to transport guests to his villa, liked to surround himself with young people, gave them gifts, and even paid their
hotel bills. When one of his guests expressed a desire for truf-
fles, he sent his private plane at one o'clock in the morning to
Rome to pick up this delicacy.

His sons became alarmed at the prodigious spending, and
hired lawyers in an attempt to curb him. He announced that
he would get his revenge by gambling away their inherit-
ance, went to the casino, but wound up the evening by winning one million francs. He died not long afterward, and the
reason for his wild spree became known. He had kept to himself the information that he was dying of leukemia and
wanted one last fling before his death.

A current big bettor at Monte Carlo is Romeo Bavera, who
made a fortune in Venezuelan oil while Perez Jiménez was
dicator of that country. He frequently wagers more than
$100,000 a night, and is a steady patron at the gaming tables.

One of the most modest bettors who played at the Monte
Carlo Casino was Prince Philip, now Duke of Edinburgh,

the husband of Queen Elizabeth. In the spring of 1947 he was visiting his aunt, the Marchioness of Milford-Haven, in her villa in Upper Cannes. Prince Philip at that time was a naval officer, his pay was modest and he had no personal fortune. He and some fellow officers, wearing civilian clothes, would go occasionally to the casino, but he rarely bet more than a few francs at any time.

Prince Philip became friendly with Félix, the noted Cannes innkeeper, who was the manager of a restaurant then, and the young prince would eat his breakfast there. Félix often would lend the prince his bicycle to ride back to the villa. Later that year, Prince Philip invited Félix to his wedding to Princess Elizabeth, but the discreet restaurant owner did not attend "in order not to vex many of my clients who had not been invited." He did send a wedding present, a tiny golden bicycle with moving parts, a diamond for a headlight, and a ruby for a taillight. He received a warm personal letter of thanks from Prince Philip.

One of the sights in Monte Carlo each morning is the rush of the little bettors when the casino opens its doors at 10 A.M. They are admitted into the large front room, which, as has been noted, is known locally as "The Kitchen," where the minimum bet is lower than in the private salons. Some people refer to these players as "the mice." The regulation four croupiers are stationed at each table, and they are under strict instructions to offer the same polite service, even though these players rarely tip the croupiers. Most of them are system players, and all have their dream of finding a magic way of predicting the unpredictable wheel and moving up in the world to the more elegant salons in the back of the casino.

CHAPTER 13

Backstage

Ever since François Blanc organized the Sea Bathing Society in 1863, the Monte Carlo Casino has been more than just a gaming house: it owns fine hotels, restaurants, beach clubs, country clubs, all designed for the pleasure of casino patrons and requiring an intricate network of protection. Since the resort area also attracts hundreds of thousands of visitors yearly, Monaco itself needs a similar system. To show what goes on behind the scenes and how it performs, Ernest Pigazza, the head of the Monte Carlo Interior Service, and officials of the Sûreté Publique of Monaco agreed to conduct a tour of their operations.

Every morning, before the casino opens for the day, four employees—a detective, an engineer, a cleaner and a supervisor—meet in the lobby and enter the salons together. Their task is to see that all gambling equipment is in perfect order.

Each roulette wheel is lifted from its pivot, and the bedding is examined to determine whether it is clean and well oiled. The wheel balance is measured with a spirit level, and any necessary adjustments are made. If the wheel remains tilted by as much as one tenth of a millimeter, it is replaced and taken to the workshop in the basement. The days when a canny Scotsman like Jaggers could find a wheel off balance and win a fortune are over. The ivory balls are examined and measured; constant play reduces their size, and they are replaced. The croupiers' rakes also are scrutinized. At the card tables the dealing boxes, called shoes, are inspected. The casino not only maintains its own workshop to repair its equipment, but it also now manufactures its own roulette wheels and cylinders.

The chips used in the casino, though, are manufactured on the outside by a French concern that supplies most of the European casinos. Monte Carlo uses an exclusive design and boasts that its chips are as difficult to duplicate as a bank note.

"Every evening after closing time, a procession of footmen come up from the caves in single file," Mr. Pigazza said. "In front of each table they deposit a wooden brown box that contains two million francs' worth of chips for the following day."

According to an old custom, a thin piece of paper is inserted into the lock of every box. When each box is opened in the morning, this piece of paper must be intact. If it is torn, someone has tried to tamper with the lock overnight, and an immediate investigation is held. The security director said this had happened twice in the last decade. A count showed that no chips had been taken.

Asked what happens if a table loses the two million in chips to a lucky gambler, he replied, "In the early years, we made him feel that he had broken the bank. We even would cover the table with black crepe as a sign of mourning. Apparently, this was considered good publicity. Today, the croupier simply rings a bell and a fresh supply is brought up right away. Our main rule now is that the games must not be interrupted."

The casino does not reveal the exact amount of cash it keeps in its vaults at all times, but the security director did say that it was sufficient to cover several hundred million francs' worth of chips. "If that's not enough, we can get more money from a bank around the corner." He paused, and then added, "But that situation never has arisen so far."

The croupiers arrive at the casino shortly before ten o'clock. Most of them are native Monégasques, who usually have worked their way up to these trusted posts. Every two years the casino conducts a course for new applicants, and their training is so thorough that they are hired by other casinos all over the world. They must have knowledge of at least one other language besides French, their entire family background is carefully scrutinized and their schooling takes from six to eight months, including a "disaster course," where everything goes wrong. The final trial is in the public rooms.

All croupiers in Monte Carlo have to abide by strict rules of discipline that are rigidly maintained. They are forbidden to have any contacts with clients outside the casino, and cannot accept gifts or invitations. The exception is the tips left by lucky gamblers, which are placed in the *cagnotte,* a slot in the table. These boxes are emptied once a month and the contents divided among the entire personnel. Croupiers are not even allowed to talk to strangers on the street.

Many years ago, a young croupier was stopped by American financier John Pierpont Morgan, who asked him for directions to the nearest pharmacy. The next morning when he arrived at the casino, the croupier was called to the office of Camille Blanc and questioned closely by the casino director, who often mounted the roof and scanned the streets with a telescope to keep tabs on his help.

During the 1930's, the casino reverted to using gold pieces instead of chips at the gaming tables, but quickly gave up the practice when it discovered that many of its croupiers were developing an irresistible urge to scratch their necks. Each time they did so, a 20-franc gold coin would slide down the back of their shirts. First-time visitors to the casino are always surprised at the large size of the chips used; they were deliberately designed that big to prevent croupiers from trying to palm one. In addition, the croupiers wear special suits that contain no pockets.

Each table is supervised by a *chef de parti,* who keeps a sharp watch on both the employees and the patrons, and these men are noted for seldom missing a trick. They, in turn, are watched by inspectors of the Service de l'Intérieur, and there is still an additional force of fifty house detectives, who roam about, keeping an eye on the gamblers, attendants, guards, waiters and grooms.

Mr. Pigazza smiled briefly when he added that this did not quite end the security check inside the casino. The detectives are kept on their toes by a squad of plain-clothes men, who supervise them, and finally, the casino employs a force of secret agents.

These men are called "the occults" by the remainder of the staff because their identity is a complete secret to all casino employees with the exception of Director Alfred Rose and Mr. Pigazza. They dress and act like tourists, and often catch swindlers in the act, since there are always people who will try to beat the casino by illegal means.

A favorite trick still in use is referred to as *"la poussette"* by croupiers. It is used by elderly women who usually empty the contents of their handbags in front of them when they sit down at a table. These include such items as a lighter, a cigarette case and a compact. If the woman has placed a bet on black and red wins, she will use her elbow to push one of her spread-out items against the chip and shove it into red while the croupier is busy elsewhere. If a croupier spots this, he will pay off the bet unless he has caught her directly in the act, but will signal an inspector, who will station himself next to the woman. If she tries to repeat the maneuver, she will be barred from the casino.

No visitor is allowed to pick up anything from the floor in the gaming rooms. Even if he drops a chip, he must ask an attendant to pick it up for him. This is done to protect other gamblers who may have dropped some chips in the excitement of the play.

One woman put special adhesive material on the soles of her shoes, and whenever she saw a chip fall to the floor she would put her foot on it and remain still until she was certain the owner had not noticed his loss. She then would go to the rest room and remove it. Her career was short-lived, though: she was observed by an inspector.

The casino's force rarely makes arrests and prosecutes only if there is a well-organized scheme by professional crooks; it usually tries to avoid any public scandal. Where no arrest is made, the visitor is escorted outside the casino and can never return. A special file contains the names of all cheats barred by the casino and a full description of their operations.

A compulsive gambler who wants to break the habit can also bar himself from the casino by asking to be placed on a special list. Once he does so, no amount of pleading will induce the casino to admit him.

In the casino's early days, a gang of thieves smuggled a small bomb into the gaming rooms and placed it under a large, lady's hat that had been left on a chair. During the panic after the explosion, the crooks managed to loot several of the open cashboxes.

Since then all hats, brief cases and similar items must be left in the cloakroom, and all the cashboxes on the gaming tables now are connected by pneumatic tubes to a basement vault. At the slightest sign of trouble, the croupier presses a button and the contents of his till drop out of sight. The casino also maintains its own generating system on a stand-by basis; it automatically switches on if the regular power service breaks down, or if a thief cuts the wire.

The finance office is on the first floor, at the end of a long corridor, deliberately designed to be so narrow that only one person can approach at a time. This prevents a concerted frontal attack on the office. Even if a gang successfully shot its way out of the building, Pigazza pointed out, the members could not get far. There is no airfield in Monaco, and the three *corniches,* the highways leading in and out of Monaco, can be blocked by police within three minutes. The casino seems to be guarded with as much vigilance as Fort Knox.

The casino force is completely separate from the regular Monaco police department, but they do work in close cooperation. If a black-listed cheat returns, even many years later, the casino notifies the local police force, and the visitor packs hurriedly after a call from a trooper.

The casino obtains the name of every visitor to its gaming rooms, and each night this list is sent to the Sûreté Publique, which carefully checks the register against its own files of criminals. These files contain the names of all persons convicted of a crime in France or wanted by French police or by Interpol, the international police organization.

The principality has a treaty with France that provides that it will turn over all wanted persons to French police; this also includes those wanted by the international police. Those who have police records but are not on the wanted list are directed to leave Monaco by noon. "The Sûreté believes in acts, not words," its director explained.

When important galas are held at the Sporting Club, the Monaco Sûreté takes over police protection and even obtains additional officers from neighboring French departments. These events will bring as many at 1,500 guests to

Monte Carlo, a great number of whom are listed in the
Almanach de Gotha, with the women visitors wearing jewels
valued in the millions of dollars. A special squad of plain-
clothes men are assigned to duty inside the club. In this
instance, the police expression "plain-clothes man," is a mis-
nomer. The officers are impeccably attired in tuxedos or full-
dress suits, and many are seated as guests at strategically
located tables. Since many of the guests are frequent visitors
there, the appearance of an unfamiliar face is a danger signal
to the plain-clothes men; discreet but immediate inquiries
are made, and the stranger is kept under close surveillance
until satisfactory identification is obtained.

In November, 1962, Monaco police took part in a dragnet operation against a gang of international art thieves believed to have been responsible for the looting of masterpieces
from museums in Siena, Rome, Palermo and Saint-Tropez.
Interpol received information that the stolen paintings
were being hidden among innocent-appearing merchan-
dise at the gang's secret headquarters, somewhere on the
French Riviera. The plan was to ship the stolen art treasures
to the Far East and South America. An American art thief,
known as Eddie the Brush and wanted by the FBI, was
believed to be the mastermind of the gang.

The Sûreté Publique promptly clamped down on all shipments moving in and out of the principality, searching all cars
and trucks, as well as fishing boats in its territorial waters.
Two weeks later, on November 15, French Minister of Culture André Malraux received an anonymous letter revealing
the cache of fifty-six valuable paintings that had been stolen
from the Musée de l'Annonciade, in Saint-Tropez, the previous year. The paintings were recovered intact. The thieves
were so bottled up that they had had to get rid of the stolen
art treasures.

Because of its stringent control system, the Sûreté often

picks up embezzlers who have made the mistake of heading for the principality as a place of safety. All visitors, whether they realize it or not, are under close observation by everybody who works in public places, and all gossip funnels into police headquarters, where it is sifted for significant clues.

Hans Juergen Miss appeared to be another typical West German tourist on his arrival in September, 1960, at the Hôtel Métropole. He was a balding, rather timid young man, who wore inexpensive ready-made clothes and heavy shoes. Despite this appearance, though, he soon turned out to be a heavy spender. On his first day, he sat down in the grand salon Louis XV and ordered an entire can of caviar for himself. He drank only champagne, and tipped a porter lavishly each time he called for a taxi.

His very actions put him on the suspect list. Not only are lavish tippers out of style in Monte Carlo today, but it is considered in bad taste to overtip unless the tipper is a very well-known wealthy person. Since Herr Miss did not fit into this category, immediate inquiries began. Casino files were checked, and showed that he had never made a previous visit; his name was not connected with any of the many new foreign companies that have been established in Monaco. Calls were made to Germany, but he was not known in executive circles there. He was kept under close secret surveillance, but allowed to continue unhindered.

He gambled heavily in the casino and lost. On the third morning of his stay, he went to the most expensive shop in town and purchased a camera, a tennis racket and tennis clothes.

The inquiries started by the Sûreté Publique produced action on the sixth day of his visit. Interpol reported that police in Frankfurt were seeking a railroad employee who had disappeared at the same time that $42,500 had vanished from the station safe. Herr Miss was the wanted man. When taken into custody, he told police that his doctors had informed him that his recent headaches were due to brain cancer and that he had less than a year to live. He was a minor railroad employee, earning only $150 a month, and he decided he wanted a taste of life before dying. He stole the money and came to Monte Carlo for his spree. He had spent $16,000 in his six days there. Monaco police, feeling sorry for the little man, placed him in a special cell containing white bed sheets, a shower and a radio until he was turned over to German police.

"Monaco is no place for people who don't fit in the picture," a police official remarked. "Few criminals succeed in trying to pose as men of the world. There are nearly always little telltale signs, and they are spotted here faster than anywhere else. I am afraid that Monte Carlo is a real trap for such people."

Although the casino is too closely guarded to tempt robbers, the many exclusive jewelry shops in Monte Carlo make an attractive target, and now and then there is a successful holdup. The latest occurred in September, 1961, within 200 yards of the casino, when three masked men rushed into the store shortly after it opened, and the only person there was the woman manager. They had scooped up gems valued at $500,000 when a bellboy from the Hôtel de Paris entered. They tied him up and fled into a waiting car, leaving behind more than three million dollars in other jewels. The bellboy's shouts were heard, and the alarm was given within two minutes after the stickup. Police promptly blocked all the highways, but the thieves had anticipated them. Their stolen car was later found in front of Radio Monte Carlo. They had crossed through an empty field into France and made their escape. The Riviera has always been plagued by burglars who loot villas while their owners are out, and insurance rates are steep.

Monte Carlo has become more prudish since the days of the great demimondaines and openly frowns upon the use of the casino as a happy hunting ground for girls on the loose, but it is caught now in the middle of a vice scandal spreading along the Riviera, including old-fashioned white slavers returning to business.

Behind this blossoming of vice is the controversial "Lex Richard," the law that abolished all houses of prostitution in France. Italy also closed its bordellos in 1956. With Western Europe booming because of the Common Market, the Riviera has become the Continent's favorite playground, and where people go to play, vice is sure to follow—a string of clandestine brothels have opened up along the French seacoast. Many of these are operated by rival Marseille gangs—Marseille has long been noted for its vicious underworld—and they have introduced typical gangster methods into their operations, forcing many roadside inns or lonely hotels in the hills to become part of the ring.

The gangs supply girls to these places for a fee that ranges from $2,000 to $4,000 a girl, depending upon her age and looks, and the innkeepers are given a cut of the girl's earnings. The girls usually appear on the hotel records as waitresses, and the owner simply disclaims any knowledge of their activities on their own time.

Many of these girls are being forced into prostitution. On November 9, 1962, a 20-year-old girl hired as a waitress in a hotel near Saint-Tropez managed to escape and revealed to police that a secret boudoir had been constructed behind the bar's washstand. In the arrests that followed, the head of the ring was found to be a wealthy man living in a $200,000 villa near the hotel.

Monaco police have managed to keep such brothels from operating in Monte Carlo, one reason being that land is simply too expensive in the principality for any owner to take

the risk of having his property confiscated, but many do
exist right across its borders, in Cap-d'Ail, Cap-Martin and
Beausoleil, and the girls often come to Monte Carlo looking
for customers. Some of them even hired out as female caddies
on the Monte Carlo golf course, located on French territory,
and dropped discreet hints of their availability. Since these
girls take their customers over the border, there is little the
Sûreté Publique can do to stop them, but they do keep a
sharp eye on all young and beautiful women who register
alone at a Monte Carlo hotel.

One such visitor registered at one of the fine hotels as a
professional painter, and she brought along a dozen canvases,
which she hung up in her room as samples of her art work.
Hotel porters noticed that there was a steady parade of men
to her room, all on the pretext that they were interested in
purchasing one of her pictures. She was exposed when a
Monaco police inspector visited her room, thrust a paint-
brush into her hand and asked her to paint the scene outside her window for him. Her expensive wardrobe and luggage had been furnished by a Marseille syndicate.

Monaco police are now co-operating with the French authorities in using a new system of identification in their
struggle against the Riviera vice rings. Girls can change their
appearances with almost lightning rapidity, with the popularity of wigs and the new, easy home-rinse hair dyes, but
French criminologist Pierre Canonge has introduced a new fil-
ing system that lists in detail facial and hand mannerisms,
favorite expressions, and other habits that are give-aways.
There are hundreds of these girls now listed in the Sûreté
files.

A Cuban playboy introduced a new note into the vice picture. He organized a stag party for fellow gamblers who did
not find the casino exciting enough, and rented an isolated
villa that once had belonged to one of the Romanovs. He

limited his guests to twenty-four, with an admission fee of $500 each.

The party opened with a champagne dinner, during which a string quartet played. Midway during the meal, a young lady wearing little more than earrings stepped out of a large floral centerpiece. She was introduced as Angelica.

The host proposed a roulette game; a wheel had been set up in the living room. Angelica held a slip of paper in her hand. If the number written on the slip came up on the wheel, the lucky gambler would win not only the game, but the favors of Angelica as well.

The minimum bet was 10,000 francs each round. The wheel kept spinning, but Angelica's number did not come up, and neither did the numbers most players were betting on. Finally the ball dropped into No. 7, and the girl announced that it was the number on her slip. The Cuban playboy was the winner. As the other guests were congratulating their host, a squad of Monaco officers stepped out from their hiding place in the villa. They showed the gamblers that they had been playing with a rigged wheel, and informed them that Angelica was really their host's wife. The couple had used this same scheme to fleece players at other casinos. Monte Carlo police had been alerted, and had been ready and waiting.

Although occasional raids will catch the small fry, few of the vice lords are ever trapped. Monaco police are certain right now that a British subject who drives around in a Rolls-Royce heads one of the largest rings in southern France, but although he has been stopped repeatedly and his car searched no incriminating evidence has ever been found against him. He moves about in the best social circles and plays regularly at the casino. Perhaps a reader will brush shoulders with him there.

CHAPTER 14

The Stubborn Prince

Philosophers and scientists who have debated for generations what would happen when an irresistible force met an immovable object had their answer when President Charles de Gaulle and Prince Rainier III collided head on in October, 1962, in a dispute between France and Monaco. The answer: very little. Many newspapers all over the world had freely predicted that tiny Monaco would disappear as a principality and that Prince Rainier would be forced off his throne. Even as they were making these predictions, quiet negotiations were going on to settle the differences.

What these prophets of doom failed to consider was that Prince Rainier is a Grimaldi, and although this ruling family has had a generous and frequent infusion of good common blood it apparently in no way has diluted one characteristic of the Grimaldi family: a stubborn will that has enabled it to hold fast to its throne for almost 700 years, while mighty empires have toppled. Prince Rainier, the thirty-second royal Grimaldi ruler, probably would be the first to admit that he also is a stubborn Grimaldi, particularly where the throne is involved.

The first of his ancestors to rule the Rock was Francesco Grimaldi, a Genoese nobleman who served under the Guelphs. The port of Monaco, guarded by a fortress perched on top of the Rock, was needed to protect Genoa from its enemies, the Ghibellines. Direct frontal assault on the fortress was impossible; a ruse was needed, and Francesco provided one. On the night of January 8, 1297, when a mistral was blowing, he appeared at the gates disguised as a monk, and asked for shelter. The unsuspecting guards, failing to notice his followers carefully hidden in the shadows, swung open the barred entrance, and the fortress fell. Monaco has remained in the hands of the Grimaldis ever since, except for a brief period when it was forcibly united with revolutionary France and its name changed to Fort Hercules. The Treaty of Paris returned Monaco to the Grimaldis.

The principality's archives contain a story, probably apocryphal, that one night in March, 1815, Honoré IV was hurrying home to his restored land when his post chaise, with four fresh horses, was stopped by soldiers not far from Cannes. A man wearing the uniform of a general asked for the loan of two of the horses. Honoré refused, and out of the darkness a short man came up and asked him where he was going. "To Monaco," Honoré replied. "I am the reigning prince, going to retake possession of my throne."

The short man bowed and remarked that it was a coincidence. "I am Napoleon Bonaparte, en route to Paris to retake possession of my throne." Napoleon had escaped from Elba. He received the two horses requested. Honoré returned to a triumphal entry into Monaco, while Napoleon again plunged Europe into war.

When Rainier came to the throne in May, 1949, he found that he had inherited many problems, some of them family. His grandfather Louis, whom he had succeeded, had married at the age of seventy-six a much younger actress, and had willed to her 50 per cent of the Grimaldi fortune, plus the right to reside in the Palace. She refused to move out, and also would not accept a settlement. Rainier finally had to take her to court, which ruled that the assets in the will belonged to the Crown, and so did the Palace.

His mother was divorced and living on a Grimaldi estate in France. To the great distress of her neighbors, she was giving shelter in her castle to released convicts whom she was hoping to rehabilitate. One of those she later brought to her home was the notorious Ilse Koch, the "Bitch of Buchenwald," who had made lampshades from the skins of victims in that Nazi horror camp, but when local veterans learned of it they protested so bitterly that Ilse was sent back to Germany.

Even his sister Antoinette added to his woes when he learned that she was trying to stir up sympathy to have her son placed on the throne. When he temporarily banned her from Monaco, she is said to have replied that she would depart on foot, and be out of his country in exactly four minutes.

But these were minor annoyances compared to the condition of the treasury. Once again there was the familiar boom-and-bust cycle of the Monte Carlo Casino. After the unexpected and large profits during World War II, casino business had dropped sharply. There was no time for play in war-devastated Europe; nations had to rebuild. England and other countries sharply limited the amount of money any citizen could take out of the country on a trip, and the bombed-out and severely rationed Continent was no lure to American tourists. The number of visitors to the principality had dropped to about one fourth of the pre-war figure, forcing the closing of 1,500 hotel rooms. On some evenings employees outnumbered the players in the casino, and conditions had become so bad that the croupiers, who depend upon tips to augment their salaries, had gone out on strike for higher wages. The casino was operating at a loss.

There were some signs that the millions the United States was pouring into Europe through the Marshall Plan were beginning to help the economy of many countries, but there was no corresponding pickup at the casino. Rainier wanted 2.5 million dollars from France as reparations for damages caused in Monaco by Allied bombings during the landings on the Riviera coast. When France refused, he called for new elections in his own principality, the chief issue of which was the French refusal to aid Monaco. This gadfly procedure worked, and reparations were paid from Marshall Plan money. France lent Monaco almost one million dollars as well.

Ben Marden, the operator of a well-known club in New Jersey, strategically located just across the Hudson River from New York City, came to Monaco accompanied by a lawyer, and offered a check for one million dollars as down payment if an American syndicate he represented could take over the Monte Carlo Casino. Even though this occurred before Rainier succeeded in getting the reparations money and loan from France, he turned down the offer. Some of the money received from France was put into the casino, and a new management was installed.

Before succeeding to the throne, Rainier also had displayed another Grimaldi characteristic: he was a well-known playboy on the Riviera. He was a jazz buff, a skin diver, a man who liked fast cars, and he was carefree in his romances. Although he continued in the merry role of a bachelor, he was serious about one matter. Ever since François Blanc took over the casino in 1863 and guaranteed a yearly fee, the Grimaldis had depended largely upon the income from the casino to run the taxless principality, as well as to finance themselves. When the casino had a bad year, Monaco also was in difficulty.

A minor source of income was from the steady sale of special-series postage stamps, which were collected by philatelists from all over the world. Prince Rainier wanted to break away from this almost total financial dependence on the casino, and sought ways to add to Monaco's income. Because of its favorable laws, some corporations had established themselves in Monaco, and he succeeded in luring some light industrial plants there.

Monetary restrictions had eased in most Western European nations by 1953; these countries were beginning to prosper, and the Common Market was off to a good start. People were returning in increasing numbers to the Riviera, and Aristotle Onassis bought controlling interest in the Sea Bathing Society, owners of the casino, and began sprucing up this aging queen. And a television promoter came to Monaco with an idea that promised to become a vital business, the kind Prince Rainier had been hoping to attract to his principality.

The broadcasting industry in France was state-run. Television, already a major industry in the United States, was now making headway in Europe. There was no commercial TV in France. A private station existed in Saarbrücken, and another in Luxembourg. The promoter suggested that a similar transmitter be built in Monaco. Linking these three stations under one control would provide a chain of broadcasting stations encircling France that would give viewers there a choice of programs, and commercial time could be sold.

He met with enthusiastic response from many business people. A new corporation, Image and Sound, was founded in Monaco to construct and operate the television station. An affiliated company manufactured radio and television sets. One of the heaviest investors was the head of the principal bank, the Monaco Banking and Precious Metals Company. Prices of the stock in the new company went up rapidly as it began operations. The idea was a good one, but it soon developed that the timing had been premature. There were not enough television sets in France as yet to attract many advertisers. In addition, the French Government was speaking out against it since it had no control over the programs of these stations, and French newspapers, fearful of a loss in their advertising revenue, campaigned against it. The manufacturing branch had sold few sets. The disappointing financial returns resulted in a sharp break in the price of the stock, and it dropped almost 50 per cent in value.

The bank president had been investing his bank's funds in the venture. This came to light when a wealthy contractor wanted to make a large withdrawal and the bank president had to admit he could not meet the demand. The bank closed in 1955 with a deficit of over one billion francs. The principality itself was a heavy loser since state funds had been deposited there. Monaco took over the bankrupt financial institution, arranged for a long-term loan from a Paris bank and paid off the depositors.

The scandal upset the Monégasque citizens; they wanted nothing to disturb their tax-free life, and with the casino again prospering, they were content to go back to the old system of depending upon the casino. They also were worried because Prince Rainier had not married as yet; there was no direct heir, and he had been in several automobile accidents. Their fretting about a direct heir went back to the secret treaty that France and Monaco had signed during World War I. Although this treaty guaranteed Monaco's sovereignty, it did contain several fine-print clauses. The guarantee was valid as long as there was an heir to the throne. The treaty also contained a vaguely worded sentence that Monaco "engages itself to exercise its rights of sovereignty in perfect conformity with the political, military, naval and economic interest of France." No one quite knew what it meant since tiny Monaco, with its palace-guard army and its police launches, was neither a naval nor a military power, and its voice as a nation was so small that it could not be heard. The clause did allow Paris to appoint eleven Frenchmen to key posts in the principality.

Although there were a half dozen or more eligible princesses in Europe, the stubborn prince showed no interest in marriage. The situation changed in May of that year. The annual Cannes Film Festival was held, and among the various motion picture actresses who attended was the beautiful Grace Kelly. She was taken on a tour of Monaco, and met Prince Rainier; they had chatted briefly once before when she had been working on the Riviera in a film being made there. One of Prince Rainier's hobbies was the collecting of wild animals on trips he made himself, and he had built up an excellent zoo on the palace grounds. He took her on a tour of it, and to show her how friendly he had become with the animals he stuck his hand into a cage and petted one of the lions. It was a pleasant social visit as far as Grace Kelly was concerned, and she returned to the United States to divide her time between Hollywood and the family home, in Philadelphia; her father was a wealthy building contractor. Her visit meant much more to the bachelor prince: he had fallen in love. Within six months Prince Rainier was visiting Philadelphia. He returned home to tell his people that the movie queen had accepted his proposal to be a queen in real life.

Gossip columnists emphasized that Grace Kelly's father had started as a bricklayer, and in doing so displayed their lack of knowledge of the Grimaldis. Prince Rainier's grandmother had started her career as a laundress, and had been Prince Louis' mistress in Algiers when she gave birth to a daughter. Many Grimaldis married outside of royalty, preferring to add vigorous blood stock to their line.

Future historians, given a long perspective of time, may find some deep significance in accounting for the actions of the press assigned to cover the marriage of Prince Rainier and Grace Kelly in April, 1956. From a shorter-range viewpoint, it would appear that most editors reached the conclusion that the marriage offered a joyous respite from the often grim and ominous headlines of the cold war. The interest of the American press was understandable: Grace Kelly was an American. And so was some interest in other sections of the world since her motion pictures were shown in many lands, but the influx of 1,825 reporters, feature writers and columnists, who overran the tiny principality, was astounding. There were more members of the press than had ever been assigned to any momentous peace conference. A solemn moment in the lives of two young people was surrounded by a carnival atmosphere that was giddy even for Monte Carlo.

While the prince and his future bride were aboard his yacht, a speedboat commandeered by photographers and reporters intent upon getting as close as possible almost rammed the royal vessel. When Rainier and the Kellys visited his sister for luncheon, their exit was barred by the press, who did not want them to leave until reporters had shouted hundreds of repetitive questions and cameramen had snapped innumerable similar photographs. One of the press representatives, seemingly overwhelmed at the historical importance of this particular moment, threw himself in front of Rainier's car to prevent it from leaving and shouted, "Over my dead body."

Nothing was sacred to some of the photographers and reporters, and police had to maintain a constant vigil at the cathedral. One lensman donned a cassock and tried to get inside the church by posing as a priest, while another pretended that he was a member of the orchestra that played in the cathedral and tried to smuggle his camera inside by hiding it in the violin case he carried. Police began a minute inspection of the building at 5 A.M. on the morning of the wedding and flushed out several reporters who had hidden themselves inside the armor of medieval knights that decorates the interior.

Impostors added to the difficulties. The most daring of all was a young man who posed as a prince. His haughty manner fooled palace guards, and he had managed to enter the salons where the wedding luncheon was being held before he was spotted by police. Quick-thinking officers, who wanted to avoid a scene, told him he had forgotten to submit to a vaccination check, "an indispensable formality before being brought into the presence of the sovereign."

They were agreeably surprised at his ready acquiescence. He told them that this precaution was "worthy of the greatest courts." He was taken to an infirmary, where doctors said he was suffering from megalomania. He had wanted to submit to Prince Rainier a vast plan for economic co-operation between the United States, China, Russia and—Monaco. The reason for his delight at the vaccination check became evident when inquiries disclosed that he was a physician.

Thousands of visitors poured into Monaco. Unfortunately, appearances also were made by thieves, who like general excitement for the opportunities it presents. The suite of a Kelly family friend was looted, and one of the bridesmaids lost $15,000 in jewels. Harried Monaco police asked France for reinforcements.

When the couple attended a gala at the Sporting Club, a young lady, disguised as the Mediterranean Sea, appeared to recite a special offering written by poet Jean Cocteau:

"The blonde young woman whom the Atlantic asked me to carry in triumph on my shoulders to the port of Monte Carlo reminds me of my own daughter Aphrodite. She has abandoned the love of glory for the glory of love . . ."

Prince Rainier hastily brought the recitation to a close,

and when he learned that a second was to be read at the opera two nights later, he had it canceled. He was overheard saying, "Who on earth do they think I am? Louis the Fourteenth?"

The press had spent so much money on covering the marriage that it took a vested interest in the young couple. Monte Carlo was receiving more publicity than it had when it had been largely the playground of nobility and the titans of industry. The minutiae of Princess Grace's life in the Palace, and such important news as a detailed description of a colorful uniform worn by Prince Rainier, filled innumerable columns. The subsequent birth of two heirs, a daughter, and then a son, was duly noted. A woman can ascend to the throne in Monaco, but a son takes precedence. Monégasques were content: there was a legal heir to the throne, and their tourist business was booming; the more that appeared in the press of the world, the greater the influx of visitors. They also approved the way their reigning prince had settled down; unlike previous Grimaldis, he had ended his playboy activities when he married. Prince Louis had been astute in adding non-royal blood to the family.

Virtually unnoticed as far as comment in print was concerned was a new revolution taking place in the principality. Rainier was succeeding in his attempts to lessen Monaco's dependence upon the casino. The absence of corporation taxes was attracting selected business firms, which were setting up theoretical home offices in Monaco. At first there was a rush of French concerns, but with the booming Common Market and higher domestic levies in many countries, an outside rush developed as well. Firms from Germany, England and other European nations, and also from the United States, set up corporations in Monaco to escape taxes at home. There was a new land boom, and since Monaco can expand in only one direction tall buildings began to dot the landscape. Although some of these structures presumably were office buildings, since their directories listed the names of many business firms, they actually were apartment houses. The business firms needed only an address; they conducted their actual business from their normal working headquarters, and so leased out the apartments during the season. To help push this lucrative activity for Monaco, Prince Rainier set up an organization called the Monaco Economic Development Corporation, and hired Martin Dale, a former United States vice-consul at Nice, to run it. Elaborate brochures were sent to business firms, pointing out the advantage of setting up headquarters in the taxless principality. In 1959, when the National Council, Monaco's one-house legislature, would not pass a budget Prince Rainier felt was necessary for his program, he suspended the Constitution and dismissed the Council, claiming his right as an absolute monarch. In December, 1962, he offered his people a new law that would transform his country into a constitutional monarchy.

The prince also set in motion a public works program to shift the railroad tracks from the shore to the back of Monaco, with two tunnels being constructed through solid rock. This would enable the principality to use the former tracks and stations for building sites and parking spaces. The refuse from the tunneling operation was dumped along the shorefront to extend the land farther out and add additional acreage.

Though Monaco collected no direct taxes from the new corporations, it benefited in other ways, through indirect levies. The new companies paid a registration tax, and a transfer tax was collected with each change in property. Funds were left in Monaco for investment.

Both the French Government and French companies were worried about the runaway companies settling in Monaco: the Government was losing taxes from the concerns that did

Prince Rainier with Princess Grace and his sister, Princess Antoinette, entering the Summer Sporting Club to attend the annual Red Cross gala (*photo AGIP*).

Sir Winston Churchill arriving in Nice aboard the private plane of Aristotle Onassis, in the background *(photo AGIP)*.

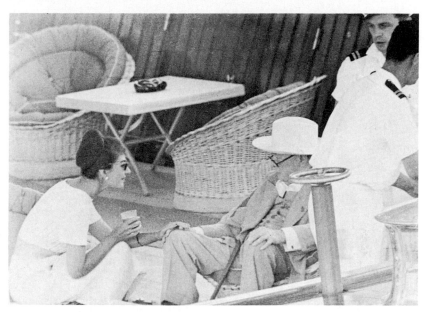

Mme. Maria Callas chatting with Sir Winston aboard the *Christina*
(photo AGIP).

Sir Winston at Cap Ferrat with Somerset Maugham *(photo AGIP)*.

Above, Aristotle Socrates Onassis.
Below, the Onassis pleasure yacht, *Christina (photo AGIP)*.

Mr. Onassis and, opposite him, Mme. Callas at a Monte Carlo banquet
(*photo AGIP*).

Mme. Benitez-Rexach offering a champagne buffet aboard her yacht, *Le
Moineau*. The author Georges Simenon stands beside her (*photo AGIP*).

Le Moineau (photo ACTB)

Greta Garbo leaving a shop in Monte Carlo *(photo AGIP)*.

The Duke of Edinburgh at a Riviera restaurant *(photo De Sazo-Manciet)*.

Fortune-teller in Hôtel de Paris predicts gamblers' chances. She is not permitted to tell lucky numbers, however *(photo Oggi)*.

business in France, while the companies that paid taxes were finding that their tax-free competitors could undersell them in the Common Market. France called into play that obscure clause in the 1918 treaty, claimed that Monaco was violating its economic interests and demanded that taxes be paid. It was Monaco's television station that led to the direct quarrel between de Gaulle and Prince Rainier. Michel Debré, who headed the state-operated radio and television system in France, wanted to gain control of the three stations encircling it, and began buying stock in these companies. Prince Rainier, who did not want Monaco to lose control of its station, signed an edict forbidding the sale of stock in the Image and Sound Corporation. He was directed by de Gaulle's appointed Minister of State in Monaco to rescind the order or France would immediately cut off all water and electricity into the principality. Monaco does not have its own supply of such utilities, and purchases them from French companies. Faced with this middle-of-the-night ultimatum, Rainier did rescind the order, but at the same time he had a heated argument with de Gaulle's man and discharged him. De Gaulle retaliated by abrogating French treaties with Monaco, and started a customs blockade. Two stubborn men faced each other, and while there were doleful predictions that the long reign of the Grimaldis was coming to an end, representatives of the big power and the tiny princedom began meeting in secret sessions to work out a compromise.

Monaco may be small, but it does take money to keep it going, and Prince Rainier's desire to sever the umbilical cord with the casino was valid. His budget alone was almost one million dollars yearly, of which $340,000 was for the upkeep of the Palace, $360,000 for the civil list, $250,000 for his Cabinet and $36,000 for the household staff.

The mustard-colored Palace has 250 rooms. It is a popular tourist attraction, and the prince receives some revenues by

charging an admission fee for sightseers; only the personal
10-room suite occupied by the royal family is closed to the
visitors. Rainier also receives a royalty on all picture post
cards that bear his photograph. He invested in Monaco in-
dustries in his determination to avoid being in the grip of
the casino and made enough money to purchase the Castle
of San Roman, which he said publicly was to be the dowry
of Princess Caroline, his daughter.

Before the crisis with France developed, palace aides issued statistics showing that only 5 per cent of Monaco's
budget now came from the casino, that between 30 and 40
per cent was realized from tourism, and that the remainder
was supplied by the new corporations and other enterprises
Prince Rainier's program had brought to the principality.
These figures would indicate that the prince had broken the
financial shackles of the casino and that it no longer was
important in Monaco's financial picture. But statistics can
represent what one wishes them to, and though it may be
correct to separate income from tourists and income from the
casino, nevertheless they are closely allied. It is because the
Monte Carlo Casino complex continues to attract the socially
important, the wealthy and the noted that many tourists do
go to Monaco. Prince Rainier succeeded in loosening the
casino ties, but it also is true that the Monte Carlo Casino
will continue to be important in the destiny of Monaco and
the stubborn Grimaldis.

CHAPTER 15

Mr. Monte Carlo

To the uninitiated, operating the Monte Carlo Casino might seem to be a safe and profitable business since the mathematical odds at the gaming tables always favor the house. This may be true of a small club, with correspondingly small expenses, but the Monte Carlo Casino is a vast complex of summer and winter casinos, sporting clubs and fine hotels, all conducted on a luxurious scale, and it cannot easily reduce many expenses. Services for its guests, no matter how few, must be maintained everywhere, and at a high level, whether the casino itself is thronged or empty. When business drops at the gaming tables, the owning Sea Bathing Society is in trouble, and so there was little celebration when the casino limped into its ninetieth birthday. It was an aging and feeble queen, with the clatter of the few chips being played in the salons sounding more like a death rattle.

The fabled institution seemed perilously close to an end: what had begun as a gradual decline in receipts after World War II had turned into a precipitous slide, with deficits piling up. The casino complex lost $800,000 that year, making the 1952-53 season the worst in its history. Yet, just one year later, there was a complete turnabout—red ink was replaced by a solid 2.5-million-dollar profit. And as the casino entered its hundredth year, it was its saucy old self, annual profits rose to seven million dollars, and four new floors had to be added to the Hôtel de Paris to keep up with the demand for accommodations.

The rejuvenation of the casino followed its own familiar pattern: once again the right man had appeared at a crucial moment. This time it was Aristotle Socrates Onassis, multimillionaire owner of a large oil tanker fleet and many other enterprises. This pattern started in 1863 with François Blanc, when he took over after the building's disastrous opening; he had not wanted to act then, but circumstances forced his hand. Sir Basil Zaharoff, the munitions king, gained secret control after World War I, but as noted earlier, it was not the casino as a business that had interested him; he wanted to use it as a lever to pry the Grimaldis from their throne and place the woman he loved upon it. He was a good businessman, though, and while maneuvering he quickly revived the ailing casino. Onassis, like Zaharoff, also had an unusual primary reason that motivated his taking control: he bought the major stock interest in order to oust the directors who were opposing his leasing some property. Since he now owned it, he promptly restored it to its previous glory, and became the present-day Mr. Monte Carlo. Each of these men possessed a personality that attracted the wealthy and the important, and where such people appear the public is certain to follow.

Owning the casino was the last thing Onassis had in mind during the winter of 1951 when he visited Monte Carlo with his wife, Tina. The couple had been skiing in the Swiss Alps, and wanted to spend a few days in the warm sunshine. One morning as Onassis was walking down the hill, he noticed that the old former winter sporting palace near the casino was vacant. The thought struck him that the structure would make an ideal office building for him. His widespread business activities required frequent trips to Cairo, Athens, Genoa, Marseille, London and Hamburg, and Monaco, with its pleasant climate, was just about in the geographical center. Following up on his impulse, he went to the Sea Bathing Society and asked whether he could rent the vacant building.

"They told me no," he said later. "I asked why not. They wouldn't give me any reason. I offered to buy the grounds. They didn't answer. I increased my offer. They conducted me to the door."

Outraged at the unexpected rude treatment and unbusiness-like behavior, Onassis decided to prolong his vacation while he investigated the affairs of the Sea Bathing Society. He soon discovered that the complex was losing money. Over the years the corporation had issued one million shares of stock, of which Prince Rainier held 200,000. The price of the stock had sagged considerably on the Paris Bourse: it was selling for less than one thousand old francs, a few dollars a share. It was no secret that Prince Rainier was not happy with the present management, and Onassis reasoned that the purchase of 300,000 shares would give him control. He instructed his agents to start buying the stock, using dummy names, and to do it slowly. He did not want the directors to notice any unusual activity, since this would tip them off that somebody was trying to gain control, and as a sound businessman, he did not want to push up the price of the stock unnecessarily.

The directors had selected the wrong man to rebuff so brusquely; they should have studied his history.

Any man with the given names of Aristotle and Socrates might seem to be carrying an awesome burden, but to Onassis the use of such names was quite commonplace. He was born in Smyrna, Asia Minor, once a Greek possession. The Greek families there were determined to retain their identity and their culture, and so they began the custom of bestowing classic names upon their children; his father's first name was Homer. And Ari, as his friends called him, showed early that he had a far more pragmatic outlook on life than the two noted philosophers whose names he bore.

Onassis got his first distant glimpse of Monte Carlo from the sea in 1923, when he was a 17-year-old penniless youth on his way to Argentina. The view of the Rock at night, with the building lights on, is a spectacular offshore sight, and the captain of the vessel on which he was sailing allowed the steerage passengers to come up to the main deck to see it. "All the lights on the Rock were blazing," Onassis later recalled. "It was a beautiful sight. I decided I would go and have a better look at the place as soon as I could afford it."

The last phrase is an important key to the Onassis character: there was no qualifying *if*.

Ironically, as Onassis sailed by Monte Carlo that night, the casino was owned by a fellow Greek, Basil Zaharoff, the man largely responsible for the youth's migrating to South America to seek his fortune. Sir Basil, the previous year, had fostered and financed a war in which Greece tried to win back the Anatolian peninsula from Turkey. The victorious Turks had taken reprisals against the Greeks living in Smyrna. Among those arrested were young Aristotle and his father, a prosperous tobacco dealer. The youth was soon released, but the father's freedom had to be bought at the expense of the family fortune. With Greece overrun with fleeing refugees, Aristotle decided to strike out on his own, and since he was too young to be admitted to Argentina—minors were allowed entry only if accompanied by an adult—he boldly claimed he was twenty-one.

By the time he did reach his twenty-first birthday, Aristotle Onassis was well on his way to amassing his first million dollars. He obtained a job in Buenos Aires as a night telephone operator, and spent his days looking for an opportunity. He knew the tobacco business from his father, noticed that only a small quantity of Balkan leaf was being imported, began his own brokerage business, and within a few years was a major supplier of tobacco leaf, the percentage of Balkan grown tobacco rising from 5 to well over 30 per cent. He also opened his own cigarette factory. Since the ships bringing in the tobacco had to have a cargo for the return voyage to make the trip profitable, he also was busy arranging for shipments of hides, grain and wool from Argentina, and became interested in the shipping business. He was only twenty-two when he negotiated a trade agreement between Greece and Argentina, and in recognition of his skill, Greece appointed him consul general in Buenos Aires.

He made his first visit to Monte Carlo in the early 1930's. He was then just another South American millionaire having a good time, and no one paid any particular attention to him. It was also during that period, with a world-wide depression on, that he bought six idle freighters for $125,000, as an investment for the future. As trade began to pick up, the freighters went back into commerce. He noticed the growing importance of oil in the world, and before the start of World War II became the first Greek shipowner to build his own tankers.

Onassis returned many times to Monte Carlo after he left Argentina for the broader horizons of the oil world; in fact, he spent his honeymoon in 1947 at the resort. His bride, American-born Athina, was a girl of seventeen, and Aristotle was forty years old, when they were married. Her father, Stavros Livanos, also was a multimillionaire owner of an oil tanker fleet. A third man, Stavros Niarchos, similarly owned a huge oil tanker fleet, and that same year he married Tina's sister, Eugenie. Despite the fact that these three men were related by marriage and they controlled a major portion of the world's independent oil tankers, they remained sharp and almost bitter business rivals. When Onassis constructed the 45,000-ton *Tina Onassis,* then the world's largest oil tanker, his father-in-law promptly constructed one larger, and the race was then on between all three, each in turn building progressively larger ships until Onassis ordered the construction of a 106,000-ton vessel, one of the largest of any kind afloat.

The year after his marriage Onassis also entered the whaling industry with what may be called a bang, both literally and figuratively. His fleet consisted of the 18,000-ton floating factory *Olympic Challenger* and sixteen whaling ships. Peru had established a 200-mile offshore limit for whaling, and when the *Olympic Challenger* was found inside this zone the Peruvian Air Force bombed the vessel and it was seized by the Navy. Onassis had had the foresight to provide for all kinds of insurance for this expedition, including that contingency, and Lloyd's of London paid an indemnity of one million pounds to get the ship released.

This was not the only brush Onassis had with governments or agencies. The Norwegian Whaling Association, claiming that his fleet had hunted undersized whales, seized 9,000 tons of his whale oil and had the *Olympic Challenger* detained at Hamburg as compensation for losses. Onassis promptly got out an injunction allowing him to seize a Norwegian ship, and filed a counterclaim for damages. The whale-oil war was finally settled by both sides dropping their suits, releasing the seized vessels and making contributions to a fund to promote the welfare of Norwegian seamen. Onassis finally sold his whaling fleet to the Japanese.

He also was sued by the United States. After the war he had purchased twenty surplus T-2 tankers. The government charged that the company he controlled sailed these tankers under flags of convenience instead of the United States flag, as required by the terms of the sale. In the wonderland that is Washington, the case was settled by Onassis' paying seven million dollars and being allowed to transfer these ships to a foreign flag, provided that he built new ships of equivalent tonnage in the United States. For doing this the government gave him a loan of 14 million dollars!

This was the man the officials of the casino all but threw out of their office when he asked if he could rent an idle building which they no longer were using. The steady purchase of shares of stock in the company went on for almost two years before the directors finally became aware of it. They made frantic efforts to line up shareholders to back them, but they were too late. When the annual meeting was held, on January 15, 1953, Onassis owned well over 300,000 shares. The meeting lasted forty-eight minutes. He did not appear, nor was his name mentioned, but one of his chief assistants, Charles Simon, was appointed general manager, giving Onassis control over the casino, five hotels, a bathing beach, the opera house, a ballet company, and assorted real estate, including the empty building he wanted for his office. He now rented it.

Onassis probably was the most accessible man of his wealth anywhere in the world. Affable, friendly, gregarious, he liked people, he was always willing to talk to reporters, and press photographers were so busy snapping his picture that he finally had to wear sunglasses to protect his eyes from the constant glare of flashing bulbs. He and Tina owned a town house on fashionable Sutton Place, in New York, and an estate in Oyster Bay, on the fabled gold coast of Long Island's North Shore, as well as homes scattered about Europe. When he took over control of the casino, he bought the Château de la Croe, at Antibes, one of the show places on the Riviera. He and Tina, though, disliked its formality; they moved into a small cottage on the grounds, and it was sold to Niarchos, his brother-in-law.

Onassis finally took an apartment in Monte Carlo, but his real home was his famous ocean-going yacht, the 1,700-ton, 325-foot-long *Christina,* which he kept docked in the Monte Carlo harbor. Formerly a Canadian frigate, this vessel had been converted into one of the most luxurious private vessels afloat, with interior paneling of rare woods and a fireplace in its library made of lapis lazuli. An El Greco painting hung above it. A marble staircase led down to sixteen cabins, each with its own bathroom, and the dance floor on the main deck could be transformed into a swimming pool by the touch of a button. The vessel had a crew of forty and carried five other vehicles aboard: two automobiles, a motorboat, a hydroplane and a six-ton sailboat. A large communications center on board allowed Onassis to keep in touch by radio or telephone with all parts of his far-flung business empire.

With his business ability, Onassis had little difficulty in restoring Monte Carlo to its leadership among casinos. It made a profit from the very first year of his take-over. He was helped, of course, by the European economic boom, but since the other resort areas on the Riviera had recovered long before Monte Carlo the responsibility for the accomplishment was his. Because of the lengthy loss in income, dry rot had set in at the luxury complex, and he had all the hotels redecorated or refurbished, the beautiful grounds and gardens completely restored.

It was his presence in Monte Carlo that was the magnet: the wealthy began reappearing in large numbers since few could resist the possibility of being invited for a cruise on his yacht. Hundreds of noted figures and celebrities were his guests. These included such heads of state as the King of Greece and President Coty of France; industrialists such as

Count Gianni Agnelli, of Fiat, and Paul Dubonnet, of the French wine concern. There was a steady parade of motion picture stars, including Frank Sinatra, Marlene Dietrich, Cary Grant and even Greta Garbo, who bought a villa on Cap-d'Ail, near Monte Carlo.

One of the frequent visitors aboard the yacht was Sir Winston Churchill. A close and warm friendship began between these two men shortly after Onassis bought the casino. Both loved the sea, and this was the opening bond between them.

"I revere Sir Winston," Onassis said. "We are all deeply indebted to him for the system of life we are enjoying. He has given that system a new extension on life; let us hope that extension will last."

On one occasion Onassis invited both Sir Winston and Greta Garbo to a luncheon aboard his yacht. Sir Winston was accompanied by Lord Beaverbrook. During the luncheon the great statesman revealed that he had seen most of Garbo's pictures and he asked her why she no longer was appearing in pictures. The actress told him that she was over fifty and did not want to be compared with younger stars. Churchill was quoted as replying that he had been over fifty when he won his greatest triumph, and added that one became old only when one renounced being young. He informed her that the movies were an art, not a beauty contest.

In any resort area where the idle rich gather, gossip is a favorite activity, and not long after Onassis took over the casino with Prince Rainier's permission, the gossips were busy discussing a break between the two men. They said Onassis had called at the Palace and had had to wait a long time before he was seen by Rainier. On a later call he left without seeing the prince when the wait was too long.

Rainier's marriage to Grace Kelly opened up a new field for speculation. Since the bachelor prince had led his own

life, the social whirl in Monte Carlo had been dominated by
Tina Onassis. To the disappointment of the gossips,
Onassis and Tina avoided any possibility of strain by discreetly stepping aside. When Rainier and Grace returned
from their honeymoon, the *Christina* left port. While Princess Grace was expecting her first baby, Tina remained in
Switzerland, returning only after the princess had gone to
a summer villa. The day before the royal couple returned
from their vacation, the Onassis family left for Paris.

But these very maneuvers to avoid discussions were causing
discussions. This came to an end after Onassis invited the
Grimaldis on a cruise aboard his yacht, and a short time later
Prince Rainier attended a banquet honoring Onassis. The
two couples were seen together after that at public functions.

For thirteen years the marriage of Tina and Aristotle
Onassis was considered a happy one: the couple had two
children, and the doting father had a children's playroom
installed on his yacht, with wall murals by Ludwig Bemel-
mans.

In June, 1959, they attended a performance of *Medea* at
the Royal Opera House, in Covent Garden, London, with
the noted soprano Maria Callas in the stellar role. Thrilled
by her performance, Onassis arranged for a reception in her
honor at the Hotel Dorchester ballroom. One of the guests
was the Marquis of Blandford, the heir of the Duke of Marlborough, a grandson of Consuelo Vanderbilt.

Onassis invited the singer and her husband-manager, Gio-
vanni Meneghini, on a Mediterranean cruise aboard his
yacht the following month. Others on this cruise included Sir
Winston Churchill, Greta Garbo and Reinaldo Herrera, Jr.,
of Caracas, owner of one of the finest emerald collections.

When the cruise ended, Maria Callas and her husband
separated. He said later that while they were on the cruise
the soprano told him that she had fallen in love with an-

other man and no longer wanted to live with him. He also said that after the separation Onassis asked him to grant his wife a divorce. He refused.

When news of this episode became public, Tina Onassis flew to New York, and on November 27, 1959, filed a suit for divorce against her husband. The only grounds in New York is adultery, and she named another woman, an old school friend, as corespondent.

Not long after the divorce suit was filed, the long-standing business feud between Onassis and Tina's father, Stavros Livanos, broke out in a new direction. Shares of stock of the Sea Bathing Society rose from 2,600 to over 3,000 francs on the Paris Bourse as buy orders poured in; Onassis learned that the Livanos family was behind the move. Onassis owned 420,000 of the million shares outstanding and needed just 80,001 additional shares to give him an absolute majority. A battle of the oil tanker kings broke out on the Paris stock exchange as they fought for control of the casino, the price of a share rising to 4,575 new francs, over $900.

Onassis went to see Prince Rainier. The two men had long overcome any ill will that had existed between them. The prince assured Onassis that he would do nothing to impair his position in Monaco. Since Prince Rainier indicated that he was satisfied with the way Onassis was running the casino, the stock fight ended and Onassis bought absolute control.

Princess Grace, who had become friendly with Tina, tried to patch up the marriage and induce the other to drop her divorce suit. Although she was not successful, a sensational divorce trial was avoided when the suit alleging adultery was dropped in New York and a new divorce action was introduced in Alabama, on the grounds of mental cruelty. The action was not contested, and the divorce was granted in June, 1960. Tina did not ask for alimony.

Since then Onassis and Callas have appeared together at

the court of Monaco. Prince Rainier and Princess Grace have gone on cruises on the *Christina*, with Onassis and Callas aboard. In April, 1961, when the royal couple celebrated their fifth wedding anniversary, Onassis and Callas were among the guests. Others included the Maharanee of Baroda; Ortiz Patino, the Bolivian tin heir; and Elsa Maxwell.

After dinner Elsa sat down at the piano and asked the others to form a band with her. Prince Rainier played the drums, Patino the bass and Maria Callas the castanets. Onassis was the crooner.

Not long after her divorce, Tina settled in Paris and became a member of the swift-moving international set. She flew to Saint Moritz to join her sister and fell while skiing, breaking a leg. While recuperating, she was invited to her brother-in-law's 3,000-acre retreat on the Greek island of Spetsopoula. One of the guests who came for a visit while she was there was the Marquis of Blandford, whose marriage, like Tina's, had ended in divorce the previous year. The couple fell in love, and in October, 1961, Tina married the heir to one of the wealthiest titles in England.

Meanwhile, Meneghini, who is a Catholic, will not grant Maria Callas a divorce. History does repeat itself in Monte Carlo. As we have seen, when Basil Zaharoff owned the casino, he was in love with a Spanish duchess and the couple had to wait for over thirty years before the duke died and they could marry. Once again, an owner of the casino, despite his huge fortune, can only wait for the woman he loves.

CHAPTER 16

Bikini Wonderland

If the Riviera is no longer an exclusive royal playground, it still is very much a playground, and as the years roll on it seems to be an even more uninhibited one, where the unusual and the bizarre seldom cause much comment. Where rank and social position once were the important criteria, money has become an even more important standard of acceptance, regardless of behavior. After wandering along the shorefront and observing the forest of yachts that glut every harbor, John Crosby, an American columnist and caustic commentator on mores, came to the conclusion that the yacht was a status symbol in Monte Carlo. And as the yachts grow larger and more expensive each year, the Bikini bathing suits, favored on the Riviera, have shrunk to the irreducible minimum.

Occasionally one can go too far, as Lady Docker found out. The English noblewoman began life as the untitled Nora Turner, and as a young girl sold lamp shades in a Birmingham department store. She was twenty when she made her first successful marriage to Clement Cunningham, the owner of a London liquor firm. She inherited a comfortable fortune of $500,000 on his death. Later the young widow became Lady Collins, when she married the elderly Sir William, a salt merchant. His death the following year added several million dollars to her fortune. Her third marriage was even more successful. She became the bride of Sir Bernard Docker, multimillionaire car manufacturer.

Lady Docker first came to Prince Rainier's attention in 1950 when she docked the *Shemara,* her 800-ton yacht, at the pier reserved for Grimaldi vessels. She was asked to move her boat and refused, until an official order was given. Two years later she cropped up in Monte Carlo headlines again. Prince Jean Louis de Faucigny-Lucinge, the president of the casino, gave a dinner at the Sporting Club. The Dockers and her young son, Lance Cunningham, were seated at a table with Jacques Fath, the fashion designer, and Ali Khan. Lance made some remarks in a loud voice, and the president of the casino sent a waiter to the table to call Lady Docker's attention to her son's actions. When the boy continued, Prince Jean personally went to the table and requested the Dockers to leave and return to their yacht. Instead, they tried to enter the casino, but they were barred at the door. Lady Docker slapped the guard. The Dockers were excluded from the Sporting Club, and they sued the casino for damages. They were valuable customers; the matter was settled, and they were allowed to return.

When Rainier was marrying Grace Kelly, Lady Docker turned up as a special representative of a London tabloid newspaper. The father of the bride had rented the summer casino night club for one night to give a party for his personal guests. Lady Docker wrote a letter of protest to Prince Rainier; she considered the closing of the night club for the evening an infringement of her right of access. When the fireworks were delayed on the wedding night, Lance turned on the sirens aboard the *Shemara* and let them howl. The final break came in April, 1958, when Lady Docker learned that Lance had not been invited to the christening of Princess Carolina. She crumpled a Monaco paper flag on her dining-room table in the Hôtel de Paris and threw it on the floor. Three hours later Prince Rainier signed an official order expelling her from Monaco. Under a treaty with France, this order also barred her from the entire Riviera coast. Since then only the yacht *Shemara* makes an appearance in Monaco. It is rented out at a fee reported to be $2,000 a day.

It may be the cloudless skies and the pleasant climate of Monte Carlo that affect some people to act differently there; Monaco's steep cliffs, which drop into the sea, form a barrier that shuts out the cold north winds and deflects bad weather before it can reach the principality. Even Greta Garbo has emerged somewhat from her well-known desire for privacy since she moved to a villa near Monte Carlo. In her appearances she has displayed a biting wit.

Salvador Dali was on the receiving end one day. He was in a group with her, and he pulled a photograph of a human skull out of an envelope and showed it to her. The actress glanced at it briefly and asked him why he took such pictures. The artist shrugged and said it was a change from his painting, and suggested that she study the photograph more closely since it was a living skull. Actually, it was a photograph of eight nude models so arranged as to give the impression of a human skull. She left the painter speechless when she returned the picture to him and said dryly, "Very interesting, Mr. Dali. But I feel you could have brought out more details if you had used sixteen naked models." Several months later Dali did make a new living skull, using sixteen models.

With so many yachts dotting its harbor, it perhaps is not remarkable that Monte Carlo should develop the first woman admiral, Mme. Benitez-Rexach, better known as "the Little

Sparrow." She is the wife of a wealthy Caribbean shipbuilder.

Whether on sea or on land, Mme. Rexach usually wears a blue navy uniform jacket, white trousers and an admiral's cap. Her rank is easily ascertained by the 20-carat diamond she wears on her cap's peak. Her yacht, a former frigate which rivals in size the one owned by Onassis, also carries on her nickname: it is named *Le Moineau*. Her crew of thirty-eight West Indians are paid to respond to her orders by clicking their heels and answering in French, *"Oui, mon Amiral."*

When not on her yacht, she occupies a large Riviera villa, Bagatelle, which she owns. One of the features of her estate is an outdoor swimming pool made of Portuguese onyx, with marble steps, and the floor is paved with tiny azure-blue tiles from Italy.

The former Lucienne d'Hotelle, she was a barefoot singing flower girl on the streets in Paris until she met Paul Poiret, the leading fashion designer of that time. He introduced her into society, and she began to sing in Paris cabarets, where she was billed as the Little Sparrow. She was such a success that she was brought to the United States and appeared on Broadway. She met Felix Rexach in New York, and when his fortune was wiped out in the 1929 stock market crash she sold her jewels and helped him get started again. He became one of the leading shipbuilders. They were married in Puerto Rico. When the once-barefoot flower girl now walks in Monte Carlo, she usually wears diamonds on her toes, and she is followed by two burly guards to protect her jewels.

The Monte Carlo Casino lost one of its most colorful baccarat players when Prince Rainier granted Monacan citizenship to the Maharanee of Baroda. The daughter of the Maharajah of Pithouara, the beautiful princess Sita Devi met the Maharajah of Baroda in wartime London. She was twenty then, and he was thirty-five. Sita adopted the Moslem faith for their marriage. As a wedding gift he transferred to his bride his assets in Europe, which included three estates in England and Ireland, a horse farm, a town house in London and one in Paris and assorted bank accounts, furniture, paintings and jewelry. The Maharajah's income at that time was four million dollars a year. He was forced off his throne in 1949 for extravagance and given, for him, the trifling pension of $400,000 a year, but since he kept the crown jewels, worth many millions, he still was considered a wealthy man.

The Maharanee left him in September, 1954, with their son, Prince Sayajimano, and took along with her some of the crown jewels. The Maharajah tried to get the jewels back and said that those she had taken were worth six million dollars. She asked for a legal separation in 1955, and three years later became a citizen of Monaco, which removed her from the jurisdiction of India and Britain in her dispute over the crown jewels. In December, 1961, she sold sixteen of her paintings at a Paris auction for $650,000. These included works by such artists as Renoir, Corot, Degas and Utrillo. She explained that she wanted the money for the education of her son.

The Maharanee always wears Indian clothes, and her wardrobe contains several thousand saris. When she became a citizen of Monaco, she automatically barred herself from the gaming rooms, since no citizen of the principality is permitted to enter the casino.

Even dogs seem to develop expensive tastes in Monte Carlo. The late Aga Khan was presented with a hotel bill of 9,500 francs for the feeding of his two favorite terriers. When he expressed surprise at the amount, the hotel manager informed him that his dogs often brought their own guests to dinner. Mrs. Joseph Pulitzer, wife of the American newspaper publisher, had a somewhat similar experience. When her pet Pekingnese became ill, the sickness was blamed on the dog food he had been eating. She directed the hotel to change her pet's menu and offer him items that tempted him. When the time came to settle her bill, she discovered that among the items the hotel had fed her dog were caviar, *foie gras* and a magnum of champagne.

Many people resent being invited to dinner at the last moment, but for a number of years one couple in Monte Carlo made a specialty of being available. Every evening they were fully dressed in formal clothes by seven thirty, waiting for a call from a frantic hostess whose table arrangements were being disrupted by a last-minute cancellation. The couple did not charge for their services; they simply enjoyed dining out every night with different people, and they rarely had to dine alone at home.

Rumors can be based upon the most tenuous of threads. Grace Kelly was a motion picture star when she married Prince Rainier, and so shortly after their marriage reports were published that Monaco would become the movie center of Europe. None of those busy with the rumor considered the obvious fact that most movie lots are larger than the entire principality, but Monte Carlo can boast that at least one important star was discovered there.

In the winter of 1951, a motion picture with a Monte Carlo background was being filmed there. One of the visitors to the resort that season was the late writer Colette. She was seated in a wheel chair on the terrace of the Hôtel de Paris and saw a slim young girl jump down the casino stairs. Colette stared at the girl, turned to her husband and said, "That's Gigi. Please get her for me."

The writer's book had been made into a play, and the Broadway producers were looking for an actress to play the leading role in the dramatic production of *Gigi*.

Her husband returned with the girl, who said that she had a bit part in the motion picture being filmed there. She was a dancer. When Colette asked her how she would like to appear on Broadway, the young girl hurriedly explained that she was not a solo dancer, only a chorus girl. The writer told her it was a dramatic role; the girl stared at her as if she were mad, and said she had never acted.

Despite the girl's reluctance, Colette cabled Gilbert Miller, director of the play in New York, that she had discovered the female lead. Her message aroused no enthusiasm. Putting on a Broadway play is enough of a gamble without hiring a complete unknown, with no acting credit. Anita Loos, who had adapted the book for the stage, was sent to Monte Carlo to talk some sense into Colette. Miss Loos took one look at the girl and promptly wired Miller that Colette had indeed found Gigi.

The young girl, still full of doubts and insisting that she was no actress, was rushed to New York and placed in an acting school. Several months later the play went into rehearsal. On opening night, a completely unknown actress left the stage a brilliant star. One critic wrote, "I am still under the spell of an enchantress." The young girl whom Colette had seen as her perfect Gigi was Audrey Hepburn, whose performances in movies since then have captivated audiences all over the world.

It all happened in Monte Carlo, the strange, the odd, the fascinating.

And the queen of the gambling casinos is looking forward to her next hundred years.

Index